FINDING THE NEXT YOU

A Young Professional's Guide to Life and Career Success

Ronald D. Bryant

HALSEY & MACON PUBLISHING

This publication is designed to provide accurate and authoritative information in regard to the subject matter covered. It is sold with the understanding that neither the author nor the publisher is engaged in rendering legal, investment, accounting or other professional services. While the publisher and author have used their best efforts in preparing this book, they make no representations or warranties with respect to the accuracy or completeness of the contents of this book and specifically disclaim any implied warranties of merchantability or fitness for a particular purpose. No warranty may be created or extended by sales representatives or written sales materials. The advice and strategies contained herein may not be suitable for your situation. You should consult with a professional when appropriate. Neither the publisher nor the author shall be liable for any loss of profit or any other commercial damages, including but not limited to special, incidental, consequential, personal, or other damages.

An imprint of Halsey & Macon Publishing
4621 S Cooper St. Ste 228
Arlington, TX 76017

Copyright © 2026 by Life Design Institute, LLC
All rights reserved, including the right of reproduction in whole or in part in any form.

No portion of this book may be reproduced in any form without written permission from the publisher or author, except as permitted by U.S. copyright law.

Library of Congress Control Number: 2025926976
979-8-9940918-0-7 (Paperback) | 979-8-9940918-1-4 (E-book) | 979-8-9940918-2-1 (Hardcover)

Book Cover by Oladimeji Alaka

First edition 2026

To my wife, Bobby for your loving and encouraging reminder to stay focused on finishing this work and to remain committed to my calling.

To my three amazing gifts – Taylor, Trey, and Londyn. You are my inspiration to live daily with confidence and courage that I may prayerfully be in your memory an example of resilience and self-belief that will guide you forward through life in your journey to discover your path to success.

Contents

Introduction	VII
The Conveyor Belt is Broken	
Section One	1
It's Your Time to Shift	
1. Timing is Everything	3
2. The Power of Self-Focus	19
3. The Journey Starts From Within	35
4. Your Path Forward	51
Section Two	67
Define Phase: Creating Your Vision for Success	
5. Your New Title: "The Architect"	69
6. Building Your GPS to Success	85
Section Three	101
Design Phase: Creating Your Blueprint	
7. The Architect's Hub Your Life Design Studio	102
8. Creating Your Blueprint	121

9. Rebuild Your Routine	141
Section Four Build Phase: Build Your Way Forward	157
10. From Dreamer to Builder	159
11. The Architect's Diet	177
12. The Architect's Field Guide	193
13. The Architect You Must Become	211
The Architect's Hub: Tool Glossary	227

Introduction

The Conveyor Belt is Broken

Finding The Next You is not about reinventing yourself; it's about investing in discovering your own greatness. To find our true selves, we all must embrace the process of excavating the treasure within that has been buried under years of other people's expectations and opinions.

Let's start with a hard truth: The map you were given is wrong. For generations, society handed young professionals a simple, seductive promise: "Get the degree, get the job, keep your head down, work hard, and you will be safe." We called this the Conveyor Belt. It was a straight, predictable path to a decent life. You get on at 18, you get off at 65, and you let the system carry you in between.

But you are holding this book because you or someone who cares about you does not want you to get left behind. You can feel what the world hasn't fully admitted yet: **The Conveyor Belt is broken and has been for some time.**

We are entering the age of the AI workforce, a seismic shift that is dismantling the old rules of the knowledge economy. The safety of the "box" you were told to live in is gone. The skills that guaranteed security ten years ago are now being automated. This realization often brings fear, but it should bring freedom. Because when the path is no longer pre-written, you are finally free to write it yourself.

This book is the permission slip you have been waiting for. It is a declaration that you do not have to wait for a title, a promotion, or approval to start building a life of purpose and fulfillment.

Why I Wrote This Book

I am not writing this from the safety of the sidelines, nor am I offering you unproven principles and frameworks that crumble the moment life gets hard. I am writing this as a fellow builder who knows exactly what it feels like when the floor drops out. I understand the feeling, the moment you realize the map they gave you actually leads you to more questions than clarity.

Over twenty years ago, I was riding the conveyor belt myself. I had checked the boxes. Obtain the degree and secure a high-quality job. I had followed the rules. I believed the promise. And then, my world came crashing down in the wake of an unexpected layoff, I found myself standing in the rubble of the plans I had made, holding a pink slip and a terrifying question: *"Now what?"*

That moment was my demolition day. It was painful, yes. But it was also the day I stopped being a tenant in a life designed by my employer and started becoming the architect of a life designed by me. I realized that security does not come from a job; it comes from the ability to build.

However, building without a blueprint and model is challenging to undertake, especially when you've never done it before. As I spoke with my friends and met other young professionals, I quickly learned that my desire for more in life and career was not abnormal. I wasn't alone; they, too, felt something bigger calling them, but, like me, they were struggling to find their way because we've all been told to get a degree, a stable job, work hard, and you'll be safe. We didn't want to be secure; we wanted to be fulfilled by a purposeful life.

Since then, I have dedicated my career to ensuring that young professionals don't have to wait for a crisis to start building. From guiding students on college campuses to coaching emerging leaders in the corporate world, I have battle-tested the strategies in these pages.

I wrote this book because I see the **"Triple Disconnect"** widening every day.

- I see **universities and colleges** teaching for a world that no longer exists.

- I see **corporations** struggling to engage and develop brilliant young talent focused more on leveraging AI to reduce their labor cost and increase profits.

- And most heartbreakingly, I see **you**, the young trailblazers and visionaries, paralyzed by a fog of anxiety, sensing that you were made for more than a paycheck but lacking the blueprint to build it.

As a young professional and throughout my adult life, I've experienced seasons when I felt stuck. Those moments taught me that no one begins the journey to fulfilling their potential with everything they need, and neither will you. The relationships, the resources, and the skills you require will not be handed to you in a neat package before you start. They will reveal themselves throughout your journey as a direct result of your courage to take the first step. Identifying when and how to take that first step has trapped many of us from discovering our greatness. This book is my effort to help you get started and equip you with the mindset, tools, and systems to guide you forward.

Your Tools & Design Studio

This is not a book of abstract inspiration; it is a practical field guide built on many wins in life, but more importantly, on losses that became lessons that helped me fail forward in my own life and career journey. For those who want to discover how to architect a life and build their way forward, this book is a GPS. We will embark on a transformative three-part journey together:

DEFINE: First, we will do the courageous work of finding your voice and defining your own unique vision for success. You will silence the external noise and connect with your internal compass, establishing the "North Star" that will guide your every decision.

DESIGN: Next, you will take that vision and translate it into a tangible Blueprint. This is where you will get brutally honest about your starting point by calibrating your "Internal GPS," assessing your skills, mindset, and resources. You will then design the systems, like your Architect Hour and your Skill Development Plan, that will serve as the structural supports for your new life.

BUILD: Finally, and most importantly, we will move from planning to action. You will learn how to overcome the inertia that keeps so many people stuck in the prison of their own minds. You will adopt the Preparation Mindset anchored in Faith, Self-confidence, Persistence, and Continuous Learning and master the art of laying your "Daily Brick."

You hold in your hands a 'Guide to Life and Career Success.' That title is a promise I take seriously. But you cannot live inside a guide. You must take the instructions, follow the steps, and build.

To help you do that, I've created **The Architect's Hub**, your Digital Design Studio. This is the workspace where every tool mentioned in these pages exists in a dynamic format you can use, edit, and track. It is where you bring these concepts to life. You can access the studio tools for free at *FindingTheNextYou.com/Start*, because I believe the tools should be in your hands, not just in your head.

Imagine a life where you wake up energized every morning, knowing that you are not just reacting to the world, but are actively building it according to your own design. That life is not a distant dream; it is the direct result of the principles and practices you are about to learn.

Whether on a college campus or in the early stages of a career, make no mistake, your time is now. It is your time to start this journey, to unlock the immense capabilities within yourself, and to give those gifts to a world that is waiting for your arrival.

Welcome to the journey of Finding The Next You. It is time to pick up your tools.

Section One

It's Your Time to Shift

Chapter 1

Timing is Everything

"Timing is everything."

This old saying holds a profound truth. Time is the invisible ink in which our lives are written, the silent metronome dictating our existence. We cannot see it, touch it, or hold it, yet it governs everything.

Dreams are fulfilled or shattered by timing. Goals are achieved or missed by timing. Opportunities are seized or lost by timing. This is not a platitude; it is the unwritten operating manual of the world. Time is the invisible current that carries some to the shores of success while leaving others stranded, wondering how the tide turned so quickly.

Consider a CEO who loses millions because they mistimed a shift in customer interest. Their failure wasn't a lack of resources, talent, or research; it was a failure to adjust their sails to the changing winds of time. They navigated based on yesterday's weather, and by the time they realized the storm had changed direction, their ship was already taking on water.

Consider an entrepreneur with a brilliant idea who hesitates, crippled by self-doubt. They wait, only to see another entrepreneur bring the same idea to market first. Their brilliant spark had no value until it was married to action within a specific window. Their hesitation had a real-world consequence measured in market share and the lifelong regret of "what if."

Consider a social media influencer with a massive following who fails to monetize that attention. They capture a precious, fleeting commodity but miss the critical moment to convert it into a sustainable enterprise. Caught in the thrill of accumulating followers, they miss the window to build a business before the audience inevitably shifts to the next new thing.

And consider the young professional who coasts through college, dedicating their time to the social scene at the expense of building the skills and relationships that matter. They treat a period of immense growth as a four-year vacation, only to graduate into a world that demands a level of preparation they never prioritized. They miss the most crucial opportunity of all: the chance to build a foundation when the ground is most fertile.

Now, look in the mirror. Be honest. How intentionally are you positioning yourself to seize your opportunities when they arrive? Are you the captain of your ship, hands firm on the wheel, actively navigating the currents? Or are you a passenger below deck, drifting wherever the tide takes you, hoping to land somewhere pleasant?

Revering and leveraging time are the master skills for growth. This isn't about frantic hustle; it's about focused, purposeful action. It's the quiet confidence that comes from knowing your daily choices align with your long-term vision. Defining that vision and pursuing it with intention must become your core focus. This mindset will empower you to maximize your potential and turn aspirations into reality.

The Illusion of "Later"

It's normal to leave college without your career meticulously mapped out. The pressure to have it all defined—the dream job, the five-year plan, the ultimate passion—can be immense, leading to a debilitating anxiety that you're already behind. This struggle is amplified by a chorus of external forces that manipulate your perception of success and your timeline for achieving it.

Family expectations, often born from love, can create a rigid framework that stifles your own exploration. This is the "stability pressure," the well-meaning advice to find a "safe" job that was a sure bet for a previous generation but may be a path to obsolescence for yours. Then there is the "legacy pressure," the expectation to follow in a parent's footsteps, which can make any deviation feel like a betrayal.

Societal expectations paint a picture of a neat, linear progression: graduate, land a prestigious job, climb the corporate ladder. This collective ideal, constantly reinforced by the media, makes any period of uncertainty feel like a dangerous deviation. Society often celebrates "fast track" success, devaluing the winding paths and periods of introspection that lead to sustainable fulfillment.

You feel like you're in a race you didn't sign up for, with arbitrary finish lines that don't align with your personal growth.

The most deceptive amplifier of this pressure is social media. Your feeds are saturated with the curated highlights of peers seemingly "crushing it." This is the great distortion field of the digital age. You don't see the hundred rejected job applications that preceded the one offer, the crushing self-doubt behind the confident selfie, or the late nights fueled by caffeine and anxiety. This constant barrage of seemingly perfect lives creates a deceptive illusion of universal success and a false, frantic sense of urgency. It is a comparison trap, a mental prison where your unique journey is judged against the fictionalized highlight reels of others.

These forces, family, society, and social media, combine to create the most dangerous illusion of all: the illusion of "later." It's the comforting but treacherous belief that you have an infinite amount of time to figure things out. It's the voice that whispers, "It's okay to drift. You can get serious later." This illusion is a trap because it frames your college years and early career as a waiting room for your real life, rather than what they truly are: the construction site.

Do not postpone the challenge of finding your way because of the pressure to be immediately successful, a pressure relentlessly thrown in your face by the false narratives of society, family, and social media. Do not lose today by believing in the illusion of a limitless tomorrow.

Success is not a destination where you have everything figured out; it is about the daily commitment to finding your path. This is a radical redefinition. The world presents you with a version of success that is just a static snapshot: the diploma, the corner office, the finished product. This is false. That snapshot is like a movie poster; it shows nothing of the messy, unglamorous, and often exhausting process of making the film. True success isn't the poster; it's the process. It is the practice.

Embracing this idea means letting go of the pressure to be perfect and instead celebrating your unique journey and progress. The pressure to "have it all figured out" is a form of paralysis. It keeps you in a state of perpetual planning because you are afraid to test an imperfect strategy in the real world. But exploration is the only path to clarity. You cannot discover your way by staring at a map; you discover it by taking a step, getting your bearings, and taking another. The illusion of "later" thrives on this paralysis. It convinces you that it's better to wait with a flawless but untested plan than to start now with a flawed but adaptable one.

Therefore, you must shift your focus from the grand outcome to the daily input. Your new definition of success is a daily one. Did you win today? Success today is not about landing the dream job; it's about spending one hour researching the skills that the job requires. Success today is not about being a bestselling author; it is about writing one good paragraph. It is the courageous, consistent, and intentional investment of your time in the activities that move you, however incrementally, in the direction of your vision.

This approach is the ultimate antidote to the illusion of "later." When your metric for success is daily, the concept of "later" becomes irrelevant. Today is the only arena that matters. Every

24-hour cycle is a fresh opportunity to win. By committing to this daily practice of discovery and investment, you are not just making progress; you are building an identity. You are becoming the person who shows up, who does the work, who values their own journey over the world's judgment. This is the only success that is real, sustainable, and truly your own.

Building Your Foundation Now

As you progress on your journey, keep in mind that timing matters as much as the actions you choose. Your twenties aren't a rehearsal; they're a time often overlooked. It's not about being perfect or making no mistakes. Instead, it's about laying the groundwork for the person you want to become and the life you aspire to create. Unlike your peers, you approach this period with focus and purpose. You understand that the time and effort you invest daily will ultimately pay off, helping you construct the life you picture.

Think of your life as a skyscraper. The magnificent views, the stunning architecture, the penthouse suite, all of it is made possible by the unseen, unglamorous, and absolutely essential foundation buried deep beneath the ground. You cannot wait until you are on the 50th floor to strengthen the foundation. By then, it is catastrophically too late. The integrity of the entire structure depends on the work you do at the very beginning.

A shallow foundation, hastily poured, can only support a modest building. Any attempt to build higher will result in structural failure. But a deep, meticulously engineered foundation, one with reinforced concrete sunk deep into bedrock, can support a structure that pierces the clouds. The work of digging and pouring is slow, complex, and invisible to the public. No one marvels at the rebar skeleton of a sub-basement. They only notice the building once it starts to rise. Your twenties are that sub-basement phase. It is the period of hard, unseen work that will make your future ascent possible.

Let's break down the critical components of this foundation, the non-negotiable pillars you must begin constructing today.

Forging Your Inner Resilience

Before building anything external, you must build your internal support structure. This is the reinforced concrete of your foundation, the resilience that will withstand life's storms. Your college years and early career are a crucial time to develop your perspective. The best moment to foster a growth mindset is right now. Look for chances to go beyond your comfort zone, welcome feedback, and see setbacks as valuable learning opportunities.

This is about developing emotional calluses. Just as a guitarist develops calluses through hours of practice, allowing them to play without pain, you develop resilience through controlled exposure to difficulty. Each time you raise your hand in a large lecture or take on a project that feels slightly beyond your capabilities, you are proving to yourself that you can handle discomfort and emerge stronger. A comfort-seeking approach is like wrapping your mind in emotional bubble wrap. It feels safe, but it leaves you utterly unprepared for the sharp edges of the real world.

You will inevitably face failures. The crucial time to learn how to process these setbacks is while you are in college, an ideal training ground with built-in support systems. The corporate world is far less forgiving. Consider two students: one who chooses projects that guarantee an easy 'A', and another who takes on a challenging research project, knowing the risk is higher. The first graduate has a pristine GPA but has never been tested. The second may get a lower grade but learns to manage complexity and deal with setbacks. When both face a high-stakes project failure at work five years later, the first is devastated. The second sees it as a data point, a problem to be solved. By actively seeking challenges now, you build the invaluable mental toughness that will define your career.

Gathering Your Master Tools

A strong foundation requires the best materials for the world we live in today. The ground beneath our feet has fundamentally shifted. We have entered the innovation economy, an era turbocharged by artificial intelligence, where the rules of success are being rewritten in real-time. The old toolkit, centered on specialized knowledge from your major and a high GPA, is becoming obsolete. A high GPA proves you can master a known system and follow the rules, a valuable skill that AI can now perform with breathtaking efficiency. Your actual, lasting value no longer lies in being the best rule-follower. It lies in your ability to do what AI cannot: adapt, lead, create, and dream.

Your new toolkit must be forged from these uniquely human capabilities. These are the master tools for the innovation economy:

Adaptability and a Growth Mindset: This is your new operating system. The career ladder has been replaced by a jungle gym, where success depends on your ability to swing to the next bar. Adaptability means unlearning old models as quickly as you learn new ones. It's driven by a growth mindset, the belief that your abilities aren't fixed. This mindset helps you view failed projects not as judgments on your worth but as valuable data points for your next, improved attempt. It fuels resilience in a constantly changing world and keeps you from believing you can't evolve your own assumptions and biases, which might otherwise limit your opportunities for personal and professional growth.

Creative Thinking and Insatiable Curiosity: AI can optimize, but it cannot originate. Your competitive edge is your ability to ask "what if?", to connect disparate ideas, and to find novel problems, not just solve existing ones. This is the heart of creative thinking. And the fuel for this creativity is a relentless curiosity. You must cultivate the habit of asking "why?" and intentionally exploring topics far outside your core discipline. True innovation happens at the intersection of different fields.

Leadership and Persuasive Communication: As routine technical tasks become automated, the ability to inspire, persuade, and connect with other humans becomes the ultimate power skill. Leadership is not about a title; it is about communicating a vision so compellingly that others want to help you build it. It's about empathy, storytelling, and the ability to build consensus in a world of noise.

You don't forge these tools in a lecture hall. You build them in the field. Don't just join a club; start a project group to build something with a new AI tool, forcing you to collaborate and adapt under pressure. Don't just volunteer as a treasurer; organize a student-led workshop on a topic that fascinates you, and that demands leadership and communication. These new master tools aren't about building a perfect transcript to impress a system. They are about forging a resilient, adaptable self capable of thriving in a world where the system is constantly reinventing itself.

Assembling Your Crew & Surveying the Land

No great structure is built by a lone genius; it is built by a crew. In an economy where AI can analyze data and write code, your ability to build trust, inspire collaboration, and learn from others becomes your ultimate, non-replicable asset. Technical skills are the price of entry, but your network is your accelerator. The quality of your relationships will determine the trajectory of your growth. Whether you are navigating a college campus, a trade apprenticeship, or the fast-paced world of a startup, your first task is to assemble your personal "Board of Advisors." This is an informal group of mentors, peers, and advocates who can offer wisdom, challenge your assumptions, and open doors.

Building this board is an active, long-term investment, and the ideal time to start is now. For the college student, this means engaging with professors during office hours, not just about grades, but about their research and career path. For the apprentice electrician, it's seeking wisdom from the master journeyman on your crew. For the self-taught coder, it's actively participating in online forums and contributing value before asking for help. It means attending alumni events, industry meetups, or online webinars, and then following up with the people you meet. Reach out for informational interviews, not to ask for a job, but to learn from someone's story. These connections, nurtured over years, evolve into invaluable mentorships.

Your bridge between theory and reality is built through hands-on experience. This might be a traditional internship, but in the innovation economy, it can take many forms. It could be a freelance project you land on a platform like Upwork, a weekend spent contributing to an open-source project on GitHub, or the small e-commerce business you start from your bedroom. Whatever form it takes, treat it as a "learning tour." Your mission is to understand the industry's culture, its unsolved problems, and its power structures. This approach offers invaluable experience, enhances your resume, and often leads directly to your next opportunity.

Finally, your foundation requires a deep understanding of the land you are building on: yourself. The prime time to understand your strengths, deepest interests, and core values is during these formative years. Actively explore diverse subjects through online courses, join clubs, or engage in volunteer work that pushes your boundaries. Conduct a "Curiosity Audit": spend thirty minutes listing everything you are genuinely curious about, from synthetic biology to historical fiction. Then, pick one and dive in. This intentional exploration is not a distraction; it is the essential work of aligning your career path with your authentic self, leading to greater long-term satisfaction and a more powerful, purpose-driven life.

Designing Your Digital Blueprint & Financial Stability

The final pillars of your foundation are built from digital bits and financial discipline. Both require you to think like an architect: to create with intention, foresight, and a clear understanding that the choices you make today will determine the structural integrity of your future.

First, you must recognize that you are constantly building a digital version of yourself. When social media first emerged, it felt ephemeral, a fun distraction. Few understood its permanence. A teenager making an ill-advised post had no concept that a decade later, that same digital ghost could cost them their dream job and reputation. The internet does not forget. Even if you've matured and evolved, an uncurated digital footprint can anchor you to a past you've outgrown. The work, then, is not just about cleaning up old mistakes; it is about proactive, intentional construction. You must ask yourself: "How do I want to be seen? How do I want to represent myself in the digital world?"

Your digital presence is the public-facing facade of the skyscraper you are building. It should be a direct reflection of your blueprint. Use platforms like LinkedIn not as a static resume, but as a dynamic portfolio of your curiosity and growth. Share articles that reflect your interests, comment intelligently on the work of industry leaders, and document what you are learning in public. This transforms your online presence from a potential liability into a powerful asset, one that demonstrates your passion, professionalism, and commitment to the game.

Second, you must build your financial foundation. Financial literacy isn't about getting rich; it's about buying your freedom. It is the bedrock upon which your professional and creative ambitions can safely stand. A lack of financial discipline creates a cage of necessity. Debt forces you to take or stay in jobs you dislike simply to make payments. It suffocates your ability to take calculated risks to start a side hustle, to invest in a certification, to move to a new city for a life-changing opportunity. Financial stress is a thief. It steals your mental bandwidth, consuming the energy you need for creative thinking and deep work.

Developing sound financial habits now is a non-negotiable. The smart time to master budgeting, saving, and debt management is immediately. Think of it as building your financial launchpad. An emergency fund isn't just for emergencies; it's the freedom to quit a toxic job with confidence. A consistent savings habit isn't just for retirement; it's the seed capital for your future business. By becoming a disciplined steward of your money now, you are building a foundation of stability that gives you the power to pursue a life aligned with your passions, not one dictated by financial pressure.

The Cost of Inaction

We arrive now at the final, crucial truth of this chapter. The profound power of "timing is everything" culminates in your understanding of this one concept: the cost of inaction. All the foundational pillars we've discussed, your resilience, your master tools, your crew, your digital and financial blueprints, are not abstract ideals. They are active, living construction projects. And the only time to begin construction is now.

Inaction is the most expensive choice you can make.

We have been conditioned to see inaction as a neutral, safe default. It feels like pausing the game, a harmless way to avoid risk while we wait for the "right" moment. This is a catastrophic illusion. Inaction is not a pause button; it is a vote. It is the active, conscious choice to build a future you do not want. Every day you spend waiting, drifting, or believing in the comfortable lie of "later" is a day you are not just standing still; you are actively participating in the decay of your own potential.

Think of your life's vision as an unattended construction site. When the architect and the crew stop showing up, the site does not simply remain in a pristine state of readiness. It degrades the lumber warps in the rain. Weeds choke the foundation. The steel begins to rust. The same is true for the pillars of your foundation. Your skills do not just stagnate when you fail to practice them; they atrophy. Your professional network does not just pause; it cools and fades. Your financial stability does not just hold steady; it is eroded by the quiet inflation of missed opportunities. Inaction is not a state of rest; it is a state of silent, relentless decay.

This decay is accelerating. In the innovation economy, the ground is shifting faster than at any other point in human history. The conveyor belt is not just moving; it is speeding up, and for those who stand still, it is heading toward a cliff of irrelevance. The cost of drifting for one year today is equivalent to the cost of drifting for five years a generation ago. The world will not wait for you to feel ready.

This brings us to the physics of personal change: momentum versus inertia. An object at rest stays at rest. This is inertia. Each day you choose to stay inactive, you add another grain of sand to the weight of your inertia, making it a little harder to get moving the next day. The passenger, caught up in the illusion of "later,' thinks that starting tomorrow costs the same as starting today. But the architect understands the truth: the cost of beginning tomorrow is the same as today's, plus the enormous energy needed to overcome the increasing inertia of yet another day of inaction.

This is why your daily choices are so critical. Each small, intentional decision, attending a seminar instead of scrolling on your phone, asking a thoughtful question in a meeting, dedicating one hour to a new skill, is more than just an investment. It is a blow against inertia. It is the spark that creates momentum. And once an object is in motion, it tends to stay in motion. This is the architect's advantage. By taking small, consistent actions, you build a powerful momentum that makes the next action easier, and the one after that easier still. You are no longer fighting the dead weight of inertia; you are riding the powerful wave of your own progress.

Ultimately, you face a choice between two types of costs. First, there is the cost of action: the discipline, the effort, the discomfort, and the occasional failure. This cost is an investment. It is the tuition you pay for your skills, the sweat equity you invest in your resilience, and the price you pay for the wisdom gained from your mistakes. It is a temporary, front-loaded cost that pays dividends that compound for the rest of your life.

Then there is the cost of inaction: the slow, creeping, and permanent tax of regret. It is the quiet ache of "what if." It is the emotional burden of an unfulfilled life. This cost is invisible at first, but it compounds silently, day by day, until it becomes an unbearable weight.

The time to be intentional, to pick up the tools, and to start building is not in some distant, undefined future where the conditions are perfect and the path is clear. That day does not exist. The only arena that matters is today. The foundation for the person you will become tomorrow is poured in the choices you make in the next 24 hours.

Your time is now.

Chapter 2

The Power of Self-Focus

It is your time to lock in.

As you find your own way, some might label you 'selfish.' They may react negatively as you step into your power. Let them. What you're doing isn't selfish; it's a vital and empowering focus on yourself. This is not just a matter of semantics; it is a fundamental re-framing of your most important responsibility. You have been given a precious and unique gift: the potential to become the next version of yourself. The value of this gift is immeasurable, and the duty to cultivate it is yours alone. To be focused on building yourself is not arrogance; it is the highest form of stewardship. It is the act of honoring that gift.

The conveyor-belt world teaches a different lesson. It encourages you to be selfless in a way that serves the system: follow the rules, meet expectations, and put the needs of the institution before your own evolution. It subtly conditions you to believe that prioritizing your growth is an act of defiance, a selfish deviation from the norm. But as an architect, you must understand this is a disempowering lie. Actual, sustainable value, the value you can bring to your career, your community, and your relationships, is a direct byproduct of the value you first build within yourself.

Therefore, we must redefine this loaded word. Healthy self-focus is a position of empowerment, not arrogance. Arrogance is the loud, fragile belief that you are inherently better than others. It requires no work, only ego. Self-focus, in contrast, is the quiet, resilient commitment to becoming better than you were yesterday. It is a belief in your potential, not in your perfection. The humble, daily work of the construction site, the reading, the practicing, the learning that builds real, earned capability. An architect focused on their blueprint is not arrogant; they are dedicated. They are too busy with the work of building to be preoccupied with the performance of the ego.

As you move from the familiar rhythms of college into the corporate world, your greatest challenge will be staying true to yourself amidst a chorus of external voices. To succeed, you must understand this critical distinction. To be selfish is to operate with a blatant disregard for others. It is taking what you want at another's expense, hoarding resources, and consuming without contributing. Selfishness creates a zero-sum game: for you to win, someone else must lose. It builds walls, isolates, and leads to a hollow victory. That is not our playbook.

We are championing healthy self-focus. This is the strategic and intentional act of placing your growth, well-being, and potential at the center of your life's design. It is rooted in a fundamental truth: you cannot pour from an empty cup. To be a valuable team member, a supportive friend, or an innovative leader, you must first cultivate your own inner strength. This means choosing to build a resilient mindset, sharpening your skills, and seeking environments that fuel your growth.

Why is this distinction so important? And why might others mistakenly see your self-focus as selfishness? Often, it's because they feel uncomfortable with your independence. When you are truly self-focused, your decisions come from your own internal guidance, not external pressures. This can be unsettling for those accustomed to having a say in your choices. They might interpret your focus on your own values as a personal slight, unfairly labeling your actions as selfish.

Remember, their reaction reflects their discomfort, not a judgment of your character. Let's go deeper into the source of that discomfort. For many, it is easier and safer to follow the crowd, to allow the status quo to be their guide. The conveyor belt offers a predictable path, a sense of belonging, and the comfort of shared expectations. Stepping off that belt and prioritizing your personal development over the group's agenda requires self-confidence and belief in your vision, which many people have not cultivated. It is an act of courage to be different, to stand alone and find your own way. Your choice, however personal, can feel like an indictment of theirs. When you start building your own path, you hold up a mirror to those who have settled for the one assigned to them. Your ambition can inadvertently illuminate their own dormant dreams or highlight the fears that keep them from pursuing their own journey. Their discomfort is not truly about you; it is about the questions your actions force them to ask themselves.

Understand that your commitment to protecting your own journey is a powerful act of self-respect. And self-respect does not mean disrespect for others. When you politely decline an invitation to protect your energy or choose to spend an evening learning a new skill instead of socializing, you are not saying, "You are not important." You are saying, "My future is also important." This is a vital distinction. Do not let others misinterpret your healthy boundaries as an act of aggression or exclusion. Your self-focus is about honoring your potential, not undermining your relationships. You can be both dedicated to your path and compassionate toward those who do not understand it.

Therefore, you must be ready for negative feedback. Don't fear it; embrace it. See it as a signpost, a clear indication that you have successfully taken control of your own future. The resistance you feel from the outside world is undeniable proof that you're no longer drifting with the current but are actively guiding yourself toward your destination. It signals that you've broken free from the gravitational pull of others' expectations and are now following your own internal compass. Their criticism is the sound of you leading your life. Your commitment is to yourself, and it's how you respectfully yet firmly chart your own course.

The Mandate: Protecting Your Potential

You have one primary, non-negotiable responsibility: to guard the integrity of your potential. This is your mandate. Just as a gardener must defend a promising sapling from weeds and pests so it can grow into a mighty tree, your potential is that sapling. It is valuable and needs a protected environment to flourish. Healthy self-focus involves creating a protective barrier around your three most critical and limited resources: your time, your energy, and your focus.

Think of your potential as a priceless seed. Left in an untended field, weeds will choke it out. To protect it, you must build a greenhouse where you control the climate and enrich the soil. Healthy self-focus is the glass of that greenhouse. It is the conscious act of safeguarding your internal world so you can effectively shape your external one. Without this barrier, your resources will be pillaged by the demands and distractions of the outside world, leaving nothing left to invest in your own growth. Let's break down what you are protecting:

Protecting Your Time: Your time is your most valuable, non-renewable asset. Each day, you receive a deposit of 24 hours. Healthy self-focus transforms you into a disciplined, yet wise, manager of this currency. This requires a significant shift. You must become proficient in understanding opportunity costs. The hour you spend mindlessly scrolling social media is not just wasted; it's an hour you could have invested in reading a book that broadens your perspective, practicing a skill that increases your earning potential, or having a meaningful conversation with a mentor. That low-yield activity doesn't just cost you sixty minutes; it costs you the growth you could have achieved in that time. To safeguard your time, you need to learn to say "no," not out of malice, but out of deep respect for your own "yes." Every time you say "yes" to a request that drains you or distracts from your blueprint, you are implicitly saying "no" to the focused work your growth requires. An unprotected calendar will always be filled with others' priorities. A protected calendar is a declaration of your own priorities.

Therefore, you must schedule non-negotiable appointments with your future self for deep work, skill development, and strategic rest and defend those blocks fiercely, just like a meeting with a CEO. Learning to say "no" is a vital skill in this process. It can feel uncomfortable, especially when you're trying to be a team player or a good friend. But a polite, firm "no" is an act of strategic integrity. Practice simple, respectful scripts: "Thank you so much for thinking of me for this, but my plate is full right now, and I can't give it the attention it deserves," or "I would love to, but I have a prior commitment." That prior commitment is to your own blueprint. You're teaching others how to value your time by showing them how much you value it yourself.

Protecting Your Energy: Your energy fuels your journey. It combines your physical vitality, emotional well-being, and mental capacity. Unlike time, your energy levels fluctuate greatly based on your choices. Healthy self-focus involves managing this fuel through discipline. This includes getting enough sleep, eating nutritious food, and engaging in restorative activities. It also requires you to be vigilant about your interactions. You need to recognize and create distance from "energy vampires" people, situations, or digital environments that leave you feeling drained, anxious, or diminished. These vampires are often subtle. It's not just overtly negative people; it can be friends who only talk about their problems, work meetings without a clear agenda that turn into complaints, or newsfeeds designed to provoke outrage and anxiety. After spending time with someone or engaging with content, do a quick internal check: Do I feel more energized or more depleted? This simple question provides valuable insight. You should also challenge the "hustle culture" myth that equates exhaustion with progress. True high performers, elite athletes or top executives know growth doesn't happen during workouts but during recovery. Your mind needs downtime to consolidate learning and prepare for the next challenge. Schedule rest with the same seriousness as you schedule work. It might be a twenty-minute walk without your phone, an hour dedicated to a hobby you love, or simply ensuring seven to eight hours of quality sleep. These are not luxuries; they are essential parts of a sustainable, high-performance life. An exhausted architect makes mistakes, and their skyscraper will have flaws.

Protecting Your Focus: Your focus is your creative superpower. It is the lens through which you channel your energy to do deep, meaningful work. In our modern world, focus is an endangered species, constantly threatened by distraction, notifications, breaking news, and endless social media feeds. Healthy self-focus is the act of creating a sanctuary for your concentration. Let's be clear about what happens when your focus is broken. Every notification, every "quick question," every impulse to check your email pulls you out of a state of deep focus. Research shows it takes over twenty minutes to regain that same level of focus after just one small interruption. Three such interruptions in an hour can effectively wipe out an entire hour of productive, high-quality work. That's why you must treat your focus as a sacred resource. Building a sanctuary is a literal act. It involves creating an environment where distractions are physically eliminated. Put your phone in another room. Use a browser extension to block distracting websites. Put on noise-canceling headphones. Communicate your focus blocks to colleagues: "I'll be in a deep work session from 9-11 AM and won't be checking email, but I'll be fully available after that." This isn't being antisocial; it's being a professional. Plus, focus is a muscle that has atrophied for many. You need to train it. Start small. Try a 25-minute "focus sprint" where you commit to working on a single task without interruptions. This technique, known as the Pomodoro Technique, is a great way to rebuild your capacity for sustained concentration. Protecting your focus means understanding that a scattered beam of light is weak, but a focused laser can cut through steel. Your ability to concentrate your mental energy will allow you to solve complex problems, learn difficult skills, and produce the high-quality work that moves you forward.

You're not isolating yourself from the world by consciously protecting these three resources. You're preparing to engage with it on your own terms, from a position of strength, clarity, and purpose. This is your mandate.

The External Forces: Your Shield in the Storm

The mandate to protect your potential is not an abstract exercise but a daily battle. Healthy self-focus is the indispensable shield you must wield to defend your journey against the powerful external forces we identified in Chapter 1. Without it, you are an architect on a construction site in a hurricane, without walls or a roof. You must understand that these forces are not overt enemies charging at you with swords drawn. They are far more insidious. They are the subtle, pervasive currents of expectation and the quiet, gravitational pull of the status quo. They are often disguised as love, practical advice, or "the way things are done." Without a conscious shield, your default setting is to be porous, to absorb these influences without question. Your blueprint, so carefully designed in moments of clarity, will become smudged with other people's priorities, your foundation compromised by their fears.

This is why the architect, more than anyone, needs this shield. Life on the conveyor belt is a life lived inside a protective structure. The system's walls, the school's curriculum, and the corporation's ladder shield you from the chaos of too many choices. But you have chosen to step outside. You have chosen to build on an open field that is exposed to the elements. This freedom is exhilarating, but it is also vulnerable. The winds of family expectation, the rains of societal pressure, and the lightning strikes of social media comparison will be relentless. They will seek to erode your foundation and knock you off course. A shield is not an act of aggression; it is not a wall to isolate you from the world. It is a tool of discernment. It is the conscious, daily practice of choosing what you allow to influence you. It is the mental filter that separates the signal of your own voice from the deafening noise of the crowd. Wielding this shield is how you maintain the integrity of your design in a world that will constantly try to convince you to build something else. Let's examine how this shield works in practice against each specific threat.

Shielding Against Family Expectations: The pressure from family often comes from a place of love, but love can be misdirected. Their vision for you is rooted in their experiences and fears, a path designed for their peace of mind, not your fulfillment. Healthy self-focus gives you the strength to lovingly but firmly differentiate between their path and your own. It's the ability to say, "Mom, Dad, I am so grateful you care about my stability. I know you see a secure future for me as an accountant. But after much soul-searching, I realize my passion and skills are in graphic design. It might not look like the path you envisioned, but this is the journey I must take for my life." This is not rebellion; it is clarity. You are not rejecting their love, only their prescribed path.

Shielding Against Societal Pressure: Society loves to put people in boxes. It has a pre-approved, one-size-fits-all path for success and grows uncomfortable when people step off it. The pressure to follow a conventional timeline, the right job, the right age, the right house is immense. Healthy self-focus is your permission slip to burn that timeline. It's the mindset that allows you to see a peer land a prestigious job and feel genuinely happy for them, without a corresponding sense of your own inadequacy. Why? Because you are not running their race. You are on a different journey. Your path might call for a slower, more intentional start, a lower-paying job at a non-profit to gain meaningful experience, or two years traveling to broaden your perspective. A person without a healthy sense of self is easily swayed by these currents, constantly looking over their shoulder. A person focused on their journey understands that the only metric that matters is their own progress, on their own path.

Shielding Against Social Media Comparison: If societal pressure is a current, social media is a tidal wave. It is an endless, algorithmically-perfected engine of comparison, designed to make you feel "less than." Healthy self-focus is the critical lens you must apply to this digital world. It is the practice of consciously reminding yourself that you are comparing your messy, uncertain, behind-the-scenes footage to everyone else's highlight reel. It's the discipline to curate your feed as a source of inspiration and education, not envy and self-doubt. More than that, it is the internal fortitude to log off. It is the recognition that the most important progress happens in the quiet, focused, un-Instagram-able moments of your real life. The person truly focused on their journey doesn't have time to endlessly scroll through pictures of other people's destinations. They are too busy navigating their own path.

Your Path, Your Opportunities

Healthy self-focus isn't about being selfish; it's about creating the intentional environment you need to prepare for your unique opportunities when they arrive. Timing means nothing if you aren't prepared to seize your moment. Living under the constant influence of external voices will almost certainly cause you to miss that moment because their path is guiding you, not your own. When you follow someone else's path, you inevitably end up where they want you to be, instead of arriving precisely where you are designed to meet your most significant opportunities.

For over 20 years, I've worked with countless individuals, and I have not met a single person who has not, at some point, arrived at a moment of profound self-assessment, asking themselves: "Whose path am I actually on?" We all reach a point where we pause and reflect on the fulfillment of our work. Is this truly my life, my path, my success? Or am I navigating a journey someone else charted for me?

Often, we find ourselves diligently walking a path that, while seemingly successful by external standards, feels empty of personal meaning. We earn the titles and income, but deep down, there's a persistent feeling of misalignment. On the other hand, those inspired by a mentor or a life-changing experience choose a different route. They feel driven to create their own path, filtering all external input through the strong lens of their own values.

This is where healthy self-focus becomes your superpower. It's the conscious act of creating an internal ecosystem where your growth is the main focus. It means:

Intentional time management: Instead of merely filling your schedule, focus on strategically dedicating hours to mastering skills that excite you, even if they aren't related to your major. This approach actively challenges the culture of "busyness," which is reactive and allows your inbox to control your day. In contrast, intentionality is proactive; it involves planning ahead to identify the most valuable skills and reserving dedicated time to develop them. This isn't about adding more tasks; it's about replacing low-value activities like binge-watching a series you'll forget in a week—with high-value investments that benefit your future self and offer compounded returns.

Cultivating the right relationships: Actively seek mentors, peers, and friends who uplift and challenge you. Your social circle isn't just for entertainment; it's a breeding ground for your ambitions. Become a deliberate curator of your relationships. Find mentors who have walked a path you admire. Build a circle of peers on a similar growth journey they are your collaborators, not your competitors. Honestly evaluate your current friendships. True friends celebrate your growth, while those who guilt you for it are anchors, not engines.

Seeking out the right environments: This could be a specific industry, company culture, or physical space that allows you to thrive. Your environment is a powerful, often unseen, influence. Intentionally place yourself in settings that match your desired future self. Research company culture beyond just salary. Do they invest in employee development? Do they promote innovation? Or do they reward conformity? Choosing a growth-focused culture can accelerate your career. On a practical level, optimize your physical and digital spaces to support your goals. You are shaped by your environment; instead of relying on willpower to overcome a negative one, create an environment that naturally supports you.

When you commit to this healthy self-focus, you prepare yourself actively. You develop the ability to recognize and seize your unique opportunities as they come. Your "moment" won't be missed because you'll be tuned into your own frequency, ready to step into your spotlight. So, as you move into this next phase, ask yourself: Whose path are you truly on?

The Permission to Prioritize Yourself

We've redefined a loaded word and set a clear mandate to safeguard your potential, demonstrating how this mindset acts as a practical shield. Now, we reach the core of the matter. This isn't just a conclusion; it's a sincere invitation to put yourself first. You have permission to prioritize yourself.

Let that sink in. You do not need to apologize for building an extraordinary life. You do not need to feel guilty about investing in your own growth. This is not an act of arrogance; it is the ultimate act of stewardship. You have been given one life, one voice, and one set of unique talents, a precious and immeasurable gift. To be self-focused is to honor that gift. It is to accept the profound responsibility of cultivating your own potential so that you may one day offer your greatest contribution to the world. Arrogance is the belief that you have nothing left to learn. Self-focus is the humble commitment to the daily work of becoming. The architect, dedicated to their craft, is too busy building to be arrogant.

In a world that constantly asks, "What have you done for others?" you must first have the courage to ask, "What have I done for myself?" This is not vanity. It is the fundamental law of value: you cannot give what you do not have. The depth of your impact on the world is directly proportional to the depth of the work you first do on yourself. To neglect the cultivation of your own gifts is the ultimate irresponsibility. To follow someone else's path, to live a life that is a pale imitation of what you could have been, is to waste the most precious resource in the universe.

This mindset is the bedrock upon which your entire journey as an architect will stand. Without the healthy self-focus to define a vision that is authentically yours, you will follow someone else's map. Without the healthy self-focus to protect your time, energy, and focus, the construction of your future will be constantly sabotaged.

So, go ahead. Be bold. Be confident. Your healthy self-focus is not a flaw; it is the absolute foundation of your future success. It is the quiet, powerful engine that will drive you forward, long after the external voices have faded, leaving only the satisfying sound of you, taking the next step on the path you were always meant to forge.

Chapter 3

The Journey Starts From Within

There's a familiar path, a script shared by most of us: "Go to school, get your degree, and find a good job." This traditional advice remains the default despite countless other routes to a fulfilling life and career.

Like many of you, I followed those rules. I earned my degree and landed my first tech job in the heart of New York City. For a while, it felt perfect. The money came in, my Brooklyn apartment was fantastic, and my social life was thriving. By my third year, I remember thinking, "Wow, I've got this. This 'adulting' thing is easy."

But then, a subtle shift began. It started as a whisper, a persistent tug on my mind and heart suggesting I was meant for more. The job, once exhilarating, began to feel hollow. An unsettling uncertainty about my future crept in, and I constantly questioned whether this was the career I wanted long-term. I didn't know what to do or which steps to take. I was standing at a crossroads with no directions. In my mind, I could hear the well-meaning voices of family and friends: "Keep that good job! Don't mess up a good thing!" Instantly, my conditioned response kicked in: Follow the rules. Dismiss this intuition. I realize now, with the clarity of hindsight, that I was allowing the anxieties of others to dictate my life. I let what they thought cause me to dismiss my own profound feeling that there was more for me.

Ultimately, I gave in to external pressure. "Maybe they're right," I thought. Why risk messing up a good thing?" So, I decided to maintain the status quo, to stay comfortable.

That was my plan. That was my comfort zone. That was my safe bet. Until that Monday morning.

It was a morning that hit you like a cold New York City winter. I walked into work, ready for another routine week, and before I could even get my coffee, I was laid off just like that. It felt surreal. My manager and the HR rep were talking, but all I could hear was the muffled, unintelligible "wah-wah-wah" like the teacher from the Charlie Brown cartoon. The message, however, was deafeningly clear.

The carefully constructed plan I had clung to for security fell apart instantly. And in that raw moment, a harsh truth hit me with the force of a tidal wave: staying comfortable is not a plan; it simply postpones the journey to personal growth.

I was devastated and terrified. The overwhelming questions flooded my mind: How will I pay my bills? My rent? What will I do now that my 'safe' bet had vanished?

But beneath the fear, a volcanic anger started to boil. I was mad at myself. Mad because I had felt that undeniable pull, that intuition telling me it was time to move on. It would have been so much easier to make a proactive choice. Instead, I was suddenly jobless, with no clarity and no direction. The overwhelming fear, combined with the sharp sting of self-reproach, was an unbearable weight.

My fear and anger overtook me. I sat alone in my apartment, feeling lost and trapped, mentally criticizing myself for not listening to my instincts. I had been so clueless, believing that following the rules would somehow make everything work out. This was the moment I finally realized, with stark clarity, that I had no clear direction or roadmap to figure out what came next. Following the rules had led me straight to a dead end. I had absorbed so many other people's perspectives and chased external definitions of success that I never took the time to define my own. It was the biggest mistake of all.

But it was also the beginning of everything.

All They Could Give

With no job and feeling lost, I started to think about the gaps in my life that made me feel so stuck. Life's unexpected changes often reveal things you didn't know before. The layoff caused me to doubt myself deeply. At first, I thought my parents had let me down. They taught me to follow rules, but not how to find my own voice and vision when the world showed me it has its own rules.

Their message was simple: "Follow the rules, and you'll be fine." But when I transitioned from campus life to the corporate world, I learned there was a different set of rules. For a time, I resented them for not preparing me for the uncertainty that comes with that realization. They showed me the importance of working within systems, but not letting those systems determine who I am.

My parents divorced when I was two; my childhood was split between two households. They loved me and gave me all they could, based on what they had to offer. After living life for a while, I have learned a crucial lesson: you cannot hold people accountable for giving you something they did not have the capacity to provide.

As I learned more about their childhoods and lack of support structures, the gaps in our relationship made sense. It gave me a deeper understanding of how they parented me. I share this because life will hit you, and you often won't see it coming. You could be doing everything you were told to do and still encounter disappointment. Our parents give us what they can, based on their capacity. Whatever it looks like for you, your success will ultimately depend on your belief in yourself and the effort you put into becoming the person you want to be.

Family dynamics can be challenging. My story is not unique, and I've heard far worse over the years from my work with young professionals attempting to untangle themselves from the pain of poor parenting. Parents have a responsibility to love, provide for, and guide their children. Unfortunately, not all parents prove to be great mothers or fathers. The journey to Finding the Next You is one of self-discovery and, above all, self-accountability. No matter how you define the impact of your parents on your life, their control over your decisions and beliefs has an expiration date.

That date is today. It is the moment you decide to take the pen from their hand and become the sole author of your life's next chapter. The pain you may feel from your upbringing is real and valid. Acknowledge it. Honor the struggle. But do not build a monument to it. Do not allow your past to become the permanent architecture of your future. It is a seductive trap to rationalize a lack of progress by pointing to a lack of support. It gives you a ready-made excuse, a story that absolves you of the complex and sometimes terrifying responsibility of taking full ownership of your life. But an excuse, no matter how valid, is a cage. It keeps you locked in a narrative where you are the victim, forever defined by what was done *to* you rather than by what you choose to *do*.

As the architect of your life, you cannot afford to live in that cage. Your job is not to lament the quality of the soil you were given; your job is to assess it, amend it, and build a skyscraper on it anyway. The flaws in your foundation do not have to be the limit of your structure's height. In fact, the work you do to reinforce those weak spots, the resilience you build, the self-reliance you cultivate can make your foundation stronger than that of someone who never had to struggle. The challenges of your past are not your life sentence; they are the backstory of your success. They are the source of your unique strength, the fire that forged your character. Do not let that powerful story be one you tell from a place of defeat. You must decide that your history will be a source of fuel, not an anchor. This is the ultimate act of self-accountability. It is when you stop waiting for an apology you may never receive and start giving yourself the permission you've always needed. The permission to succeed, despite it all.

Preparation is the Highest Form of Faith

The layoff was a pivotal turning point. In the midst of the uncertainty was hope, the hope that came from the intuition that there was more for me than that job offered. The layoff was not the end, but a beginning. I had to figure out how to get from where I was to where I wanted to be. That had nothing to do with my parents or friends. It had everything to do with me.

While recalibrating my mind, I attended a church service that unlocked what I felt in my spirit but could not articulate. The sermon's main point was this: "Preparation is the highest form of faith."

Uncertainty and self-doubt are the ingredients of fear. This is not just a metaphor; it's a formula. Uncertainty whispers, "What if you fail?" Self-doubt responds, "You will." This toxic inner dialogue is the breeding ground for fear, a sickness that infects the mind, body, and spirit if left unchecked. It starts in the mind as a critical inner voice that questions every move. The conversation is nonstop. Uncertainty, the strategist, plants the seeds of external worry: "What if you're too late and someone else gets there first? What if the market shifts and this idea becomes worthless? What if you tell people your plan and they laugh at you?" Then Self-Doubt, the internalizer, personalizes those fears: "You're not smart enough to adapt if the market changes. You don't have the discipline to follow through. Remember that other time you tried and gave up? This is no different." Together, they weave a story of unavoidable failure. This poison then shows up in the body as anxiety and lethargy, and eventually infects the spirit, dimming the light of your ambition. Many young professionals with tremendous potential become adults crippled by this sickness, never realizing their capacity to fulfill their dreams. Their potential doesn't vanish; it atrophies from disuse. The sickness convinces them that the safety of the known is preferable to the risk of the unknown, causing them to trade the possibility of a masterpiece for the certainty of an empty lot. Over time, the symptoms of this infection grow stronger. Procrastination is the most visible sign, but the deeper ailments are perfectionism, the refusal to start until conditions are flawless, which they never are, and comparison, which uses the curated success of others as evidence of your own inadequacy. It happens to us all. Life presents these moments, these forks in the road, that either propel you forward or paralyze you. The choice is yours.

Mistakes will happen. What is most important is not avoiding them, but how you speak to yourself afterward. The pain of disappointment can lead you to poison yourself with uncertainty and self-doubt. It all depends on what you do when nobody's watching; your mind can either work for you or against you. Preparation is a daily routine done in solitude. It's the mental and spiritual exercise that produces self-confidence, persistence, and a passion for continuous learning the skills you need to manifest your vision. Without this preparation mindset, failure can become a way of life instead of a life lesson. Initially, I blamed myself for being laid off. But as I adopted a preparation mindset, I realized I was poisoning myself with self-doubt. If you don't notice these moments, these seeds of fear, you'll never tap into the power of possibility. You'll stay comfortable, even as the urge to discover the next version of yourself pulls at you. The layoff was the push I needed to overcome my self-doubt and strengthen my mind.

The Antidote for Fear

When I speak of faith, I mean a foundational belief. Belief in a higher power can be a profound source of strength, but the faith we must build as architects is also a deep, unwavering belief in ourselves, our vision, and our capacity to build it. Faith, at its core, is belief not just in God, but in yourself. So, the question becomes: do you believe in yourself?

You combat self-doubt, uncertainty, and fear with faith. Think of faith as an antidote. It is the antibiotic that accelerates your recovery from the infection of fear. As you pursue your journey, belief in yourself will be the medicine that helps you develop the strength to overcome the self-doubt and uncertainty that life throws at you.

Think of your mindset as a diet. Just as fruits and vegetables strengthen your body, your daily consumption of thoughts, actions, and information must feed your faith. There is a power in self-belief that you must realize to experience the fullness of who you can become. Without it, you will trap yourself in cycles of procrastination that perpetuate the infection of fear.

God's position on faith is that you have it in him *and* yourself. This bilateral exchange is a force multiplier. Our lack of faith in ourselves stops us and causes us to self-sabotage. Plenty of people will seek to disrupt your progress; don't do their dirty work for them.

This is what makes preparation the highest form of faith. Your belief in yourself and your creator will help you achieve a life of purpose. With a preparation mindset, you wake up daily understanding that you are doing the work to prepare for the success you envision. Will every day be perfect? No. Will you be disappointed? Yes. Will you hear the whispers from uncertainty and self-doubt? Yes. But a preparation mindset equips you with the belief that it's all the good and the bad that work together to prepare you for the moments you believe will arrive.

Faith became the daily nourishment I needed to restore myself to a healthy mindset. After hearing that sermon, I started preparing for the next job I believed was coming. Not just any job, but one I began to envision through the power of faith both in God and in myself.

The only validation you need is the one you receive when you connect through faith with the creator who made you. Your faith will protect you from external pressures, turning your self-doubt into self-confidence and your uncertainty into clarity.

Adopting a preparation mindset means mastering a dynamic cycle of three core skills: self-confidence, persistence, and continuous learning. These are not personality traits you are born with; they are muscles you build through daily practice.

Self-Confidence: Forged in Private Promises

Self-confidence isn't a feeling you wait for; it's a structure you build. This structure is forged in the quiet, unseen moments of your day, created from the promises you keep to yourself. Think of it as your internal integrity. Every time you choose disciplined actions over easy distractions, getting up on time, completing the workout, making the difficult call, you deposit into your self-trust account. This is the only currency of confidence that maintains its value. External praise is fleeting, but your internal record of your own reliability is permanent. This confidence enables you to face criticism without falling apart because your sense of worth isn't up for debate. It has been earned through action. You learn to trust yourself not through reciting affirmations but by gathering evidence. This embodies the core of the preparation mindset: you act your way into belief. Taking one small, uncertain step creates a piece of evidence, which then fuels the belief to take a slightly larger step. That process is how you build the shield protecting your vision. It might not be impenetrable, but it is real because you forged it yourself in the fire of your daily effort.

Persistence: The Character of Your Commitment

Persistence is the engine that converts your vision into reality. It is the character you reveal, not on the days you feel inspired, but on the days you feel discouraged. Motivation is a spark; persistence is the slow, steady burn that keeps the fire going through the long night. It is the force that bridges the gap between your actions, connecting yesterday's effort to today's, and today's to tomorrow's. Success is a journey of a thousand small steps, and persistence is the commitment to take the next one, especially after a fall. This is what separates the architect from the dreamer. The dreamer gives up when they hit a wall; the architect sees the wall as a problem to be solved and begins searching for a door, a window, or a sledgehammer. This is not about mindless effort; it is about intelligent endurance. The resilient belief in your destination fuels your search for a new path when the old one is blocked. Persistence transforms failure from a verdict into a navigation tool. Every obstacle becomes a test of your commitment, and with every test you pass, you are not just getting closer to your goal; you are hardening into the person who is strong enough to handle the success that awaits you.

Continuous Learning: The Craft of Your Evolution

Continuous learning is the active, humble pursuit of becoming better. It is the engine of your evolution, ensuring the architect you are tomorrow is more capable than the architect you are today. In a world of constant change, the only true security is your ability to adapt, and you can only adapt as fast as you can learn. The learner's mindset is your greatest asset. It requires you to see every outcome, especially a failure, as a masterclass. When a project falls short, the learner asks, "What is the lesson here?" They see the experience not as a mark against their worth, but as a tuition payment for an invaluable piece of wisdom. This is how you turn the rubble of a mistake into the foundation of your next success. This is an active craft. It means intentionally seeking out knowledge that challenges your assumptions. It means cultivating a deep curiosity about your field, world, and yourself. This commitment keeps your self-confidence from becoming arrogant and your persistence from becoming stubborn. It ensures you are not just working hard, but always working smarter, constantly refining your blueprint with the hard-won wisdom of your experience.

Showing Up for Yourself

Whether on a college campus or early in your career, the next question you must ask is: how do I want to show up for myself?

We have all heard the story of David and Goliath. We are inspired by the young shepherd who slays a giant with an inadequate weapon and saves his country. For the soldiers who watched, Goliath was an obstacle. David had an opportunity to prove his belief in himself and his God. If David had allowed the fear of others to define him, he would have missed his moment. He was willing to show up for himself, not because of what others thought, but because of his beliefs about himself.

This is a powerful thought and even more important awareness we all most develop and it begins with a simple question, what do you believe about yourself?

We often reduce David's story to a 60-second highlight reel of his battle with Goliath. This snapshot causes us to miss the most valuable part of his journey. Before he stepped into the spotlight, he oversaw his father's sheep in obscurity on the backside of a mountain. It was there, in isolation and out of the public eye, that David developed his self-confidence.

If you don't learn to show up for yourself in private, it's nearly impossible to do so in public. Showing up for yourself is about cultivating your inner greatness, adopting a preparation mindset, and refusing to back down from challenges even when no one is watching. If you wait for an audience, you'll miss the moments meant to prepare you.

These moments never introduce themselves politely. They come like unexpected guests. Before facing Goliath, while tending his father's sheep, a lion snatched one of the flock. David chased after the lion, killed it, and rescued the sheep. On another occasion, a bear did the same. David went after the bear, killed it, and returned the stolen sheep to the flock.

The lion and the bear were his private battles. They were his opportunities. Had David defaulted on these challenges, he would not have been prepared for Goliath. While others doubted him, David was fully aware of his capabilities because he had built them in solitude. His belief system was stronger than his fear because he was willing to build it when no one was watching.

As you look at your journey, pursue the bear and the lion in your life. They are opportunities designed to prepare you for your Goliath moment. The bear in your life may be past failures that have stolen your belief in yourself. Like David, show up and rescue your future from the attack of your past. The lion may be the thoughts in your mind telling you a life of purpose is unattainable. Show up, confront those forces, and rescue your happiness.

The person who sees opportunity in obstacles is committed to showing up for themselves, regardless of who is watching. Your journey begins from within, through a deep belief in yourself that activates the faith needed to develop a preparation mindset. This isn't about your parents, friends, or societal pressures. It's about you. We aren't looking for excuses; we're seeking opportunities. We are here to show up for ourselves and choose the hard work that success demands. This is the final, non-negotiable principle of this chapter. It sums up every lesson from the pain of a layoff to the wisdom of a sermon to the courage of a shepherd boy. Everything depends on this choice. The world may have given you a tough starting point, a foundation marred by neglect, or a rulebook that led you astray. That is the past. That is the soil. Your job is not to curse the soil but to cultivate it. Showing up for yourself is about becoming your own gardener, your own advocate, and your greatest champion. It's the moment you stop waiting for approval, support, or permission that may never come and decide to give it to yourself.

This is the hard work. It is the unseen labor of building self-trust when trust was never modeled for you. It is the quiet discipline of spending an hour preparing for an opportunity while others are scrolling, not because you feel motivated, but because you are committed. Each hour you invest in yourself, each small promise you keep, is a brick you lay in a new foundation a foundation of your own making. It means taking your faith in a higher power and multiplying it by the faith you build in yourself. You become an unstoppable force not when life gets easy, but when you decide to become stronger than your excuses.

It's here that your past stories, like the struggles with your parents and the pain of failure, are transformed. They cease to be just a list of excuses for what you can't do and become the motivation for what you can. You are not shaped by the lions and bears that attack you but by your decision to fight back. The absence of a cheering crowd does not define you; instead, you are shaped by your willingness to prepare alone in the mountains. This is your moment to stop waiting for a hero and start becoming one. The journey to Finding the Next You isn't about waiting for someone else to write your story. It's about picking up the pen, turning to a blank page, and having the courage to write the first word yourself. Show up. Do the work. The world is waiting for your arrival.

Chapter 4

Your Path Forward

Have you ever felt like you're on a conveyor belt, moving along a predetermined path not of your own design? To understand this feeling, we need to go back about 150 years.

Before the factory whistle dictated the day, life followed a different rhythm. For most people, this was the cycle of the seasons: planting in spring, harvesting in fall. For craftsmen, it was the rhythm of their own making, the self-directed pace of a blacksmith shaping iron or a weaver at their loom. Work and life were intertwined, demanding but not compartmentalized. Life had a rhythm, but it was not uniform. The rise of factories changed everything. Suddenly, the economy needed a new kind of worker: someone who could show up on time, perform a repetitive task for hours, and follow instructions without question. To meet this demand, a new institution was created: the modern public education system.

Modeled directly on the factories they served, schools became assembly lines for future workers. The bells that shuttle you from class to class directly echo the factory floor's shift changes. You were grouped by age, like products by model year, moving from station to station: math, science, history to have specialized knowledge installed. The primary goal was not to foster creativity but to produce a reliable, interchangeable workforce. A wild success for its time, this system culminates in the conveyor belt you feel today. It teaches an insidious lesson: your goal is not to learn but to figure out what the person in authority wants and to deliver it efficiently. It creates employees, not innovators.

Then, you graduate and move on to the next step: climbing the corporate ladder. Rooted in the same hierarchical logic, the corporate structure was built for efficiency. The path appears clear, the steps are laid out, and the rewards seem predictable. But the ladder is unstable. First, it might be leaning against the wrong wall, leading you to a "success" that feels empty. Second, in this era of constant disruption, the entire wall of your company or industry can be knocked down overnight. This isn't exaggeration; it's the new reality of the AI revolution. Past technological shifts automated manual labor; this revolution automates thinking work. The specialized knowledge that once secured a 40-year career can now be replaced by a new algorithm. The industry you consider "safe" is just one innovation away from being fundamentally reshaped. The illusion of safety within the box is just that, an illusion.

Those invisible walls you feel are not relics of a world that no longer exists; they are the active, present-day framework of the box that traps so many. The educational system, with its standardized tests, and the traditional workforce, with its rigid career paths, are the walls. They were built to foster conformity and predictability, and in doing so, they inadvertently suffocate the very creativity and purpose you were born to express. They create a comfortable cage, rewarding those who follow the rules and quietly discouraging those who dare to ask if there is a different way. But you will not be trapped. The very act of reading this book is you, searching for the seams in the walls. It is you, feeling for the handle on a door that others don't even believe exists. This book is your guide to finding that door.

How to Find a New Way

How do you find a new path if the ladder can no longer be trusted? It begins with a fundamental mindset shift: you must stop letting the world define who you are and start telling the world who you will become. This is what it means to truly show up for yourself to become the primary driver of your career, not just a passenger following someone else's rules. This transition requires a radical act of self-reliance, an intentional decoupling from the systems that have, until now, defined your worth.

The foundational shift is moving from depending on external validation to cultivating internal validation. The fleeting high of a good grade or a manager's approval is a sugar rush; it feels good for a moment, then vanishes. True, lasting fulfillment comes from the quiet satisfaction of mastering a difficult skill or seeing a project you're passionate about come to life. In a world reshaped by AI, this is not just a feel-good preference but a survival strategy. External metrics are becoming increasingly irrelevant. Tasks that once earned praise, such as organizing data efficiently, writing standard reports, and summarizing research, are now performed faster and more accurately by agentic AI. Chasing validation by excelling at repetitive tasks is a race you are guaranteed to lose. Your unique, durable value lies in human qualities that cannot be coded: your judgment, your ethical compass, your creative intuition, and your ability to inspire a team. These qualities are not measured on a report card or performance review. They are assessed on your own internal scorecard. Here's a simple practice: the next time you complete a task, before showing it to anyone, take sixty seconds to be your own judge. Ask yourself, "What am I proud of here? What did I learn?" This simple act trains your brain to value your own assessment over that of others.

This leads to adopting an "entrepreneurial mindset," and no, that doesn't mean you have to start a company. It's a way of operating, a perspective on the world accessible to everyone. It involves seeing problems as opportunities and taking initiative. Instead of waiting for instructions, you actively identify friction points and propose solutions. This mindset changes you from a passenger into a driver. The passenger views their role as a limit; the driver sees it as a starting point. This is the difference between an employee and an "intrapreneur," someone who acts like a founder within a larger organization. The intrapreneur takes ownership. They aim to understand the whole business, not just their small part. They anticipate future needs and develop the skills to address them before being asked. This proactive approach gives you agency, the power to shape your career instead of merely reacting to it.

This sense of agency lets you see your career not as a straight line, but as a lively collection of assets: skills, projects, experiences, and relationships. Think of yourself as the manager of "You, Inc." A wise manager doesn't buy a single stock and hold it for 40 years; they actively manage their portfolio. They recognize which assets are increasing in value and which are decreasing. In the innovation-driven economy, rote knowledge and repeatable technical skills are losing value. Their worth declines. The assets gaining value are the uniquely human "power skills" we will soon discuss. Managing your career portfolio means having the courage to sell off what no longer benefits you, like the familiar but outdated skills or dead-end projects, and reinvesting your time and energy into developing skills that will pay off in the future. This approach encourages you to take a job not just for the title but for the skill it adds to your portfolio. It motivates you to start a side project not just for money but for the experience it offers. It makes you resilient, adaptable, and ultimately, in control. This is the new way. It's not a path you stumble upon but one you create. The first step in shaping your future is understanding which assets are worth investing in to help you grow.

Building Your Skillset for the Innovation Economy

Having a new mindset is your guiding force, but you still need the right tools to build your future. The knowledge economy was about what you knew; the innovation economy is about what you can do with what you know. Since there's no syllabus for the future, you have to build your own toolkit. The skills that matter most are the ones that allow you to create, connect, and adapt.

First, you must learn how to learn. Think of this as your superpower. In a world where specific technologies become obsolete in years, the ability to rapidly pick up new skills is your ultimate career insurance. It's about building the muscle of curiosity. Try this: explain a complex topic in the simplest possible terms, as if to a child. This instantly reveals the gaps in your own understanding. Make it a habit to spend an hour a week exploring a topic you know nothing about. This is not a waste of time; it is you practicing the skill of self-directed learning.

Second, develop "T-shaped" expertise. Imagine the letter 'T'. The vertical bar is your deep expertise in one core area. In the old economy, that was enough. In the innovation economy, your value is amplified by the horizontal bar: a broad understanding of many different areas. Real innovation happens at the intersection of disciplines, the artist who understands marketing, the engineer who understands psychology. Embrace intellectual diversity by reading books, watching documentaries, and engaging with people from fields different from yours.

Finally, master the "power skills," often incorrectly labeled as "soft skills," which dangerously downplays their significance. These are the drivers of progress. Communication is not just about clarity; it is about storytelling. Can you craft a narrative that inspires people to act? Creativity is not just for artists; it is about identifying problems. Train yourself to notice the small inconveniences in your daily life; they are often the starting points for great ideas. And networking is not a transactional game of collecting contacts; it is genuine work to build a community. Be more interested than interesting. By focusing on learning and giving, you will develop relationships that will support you throughout your journey.

The conveyor belt you experience isn't a new phenomenon; it's simply the latest model, upgraded through a series of major economic shifts. Each industrial revolution has transformed our world, redefining work and what it means to succeed.

The **First Industrial Revolution**, powered by steam and water, pulled our ancestors from the fields and placed them in factories. It created the concept of a standardized "worker," an individual valued for their ability to perform a physical task reliably.

Second, this model was perfected with the magic of electricity and the assembly line. It created the hierarchical corporate ladder, rewarding loyalty and specialization, and birthed the "company man" who could expect a predictable career in exchange for decades of service.

The **Third Industrial Revolution**, the digital age, swapped the factory floor for the office cubicle and the wrench for the keyboard. We became "knowledge workers," valued for our ability to manage and process information. The tools and the location changed, but the fundamental expectation did not: operate efficiently within a predefined system.

We are living through the **Fourth Industrial Revolution**, an era defined by artificial intelligence, automation, and total connectivity. But this revolution is different. For the first time, machines are not just augmenting our physical labor or our ability to calculate; they are beginning to automate the core cognitive tasks that define the "knowledge worker." The conveyor belt isn't just speeding up; for many, it's heading toward a cliff.

But here is the crucial lesson buried in this history: The innovators, entrepreneurs, and visionary corporations that *drove* these transformations were never passively riding the belt. They were the ones who saw the limitations of the old system and had the courage to build a new one. They didn't just adapt to the change; they *were* the change.

This is the mindset you must now apply to your own life. To break out of the box and thrive in this new era, stop seeing yourself as a passenger on the conveyor belt and start acting like the innovator who designs the next system. This requires a conscious, intentional focus on your own self-evolution. Just as industrial revolutions propel the world forward, you must seek and embrace your own *personal* revolutions. This challenging project teaches you a new skill, the uncomfortable conversation that opens a new door, and the side hustle that awakens a new passion. These are the transformational moments that allow you to jump off the belt and begin to create your own way forward.

Don't Miss Your Moment

Just as industrial revolutions push the world forward, you must embrace your own personal revolutions. These transformative moments, like tackling a tough project or having an awkward conversation, enable you to step off the conveyor belt. But what does that look like on an average Tuesday?

Your life constantly presents you with opportunities. They arrive in emails, in conversations, and in the face of unexpected challenges. They are daily forks in the road. The key is to recognize that not all paths lead to growth. They fall into two distinct categories: those that propel you forward and those that hold you in place. Learning to distinguish between the two is the foundational skill for your self-evolution.

Opportunities that propel you forward are the building blocks of your personal revolution. They are invitations to grow, learn, and become a slightly better version of yourself. A motivating opportunity might be a sudden moment of clarity, feedback from a mentor that stings a bit but reveals a key blind spot. It could also be joining a new community that exposes you to a different way of thinking, where their normal becomes your new goal. It might even be a direct chance to develop a new skill, like volunteering to lead a small, challenging project that no one else wants.

Identifying these moments requires focus because an opportunity to propel you forward almost always involves a degree of discomfort. It's the knot in your stomach before you raise your hand in a large meeting. It's the hesitation before introducing yourself to someone you admire. The programming of the conveyor-belt world tells us to retreat from this feeling. Discomfort is a warning sign, a signal to return to safety. But the innovator inside you must learn to recognize that feeling not as a stop sign, but as a signpost pointing directly toward growth. It's the muscle soreness after a good workout, the physical evidence of getting stronger.

Certain moments can propel you forward, but others can hold you back. These choices keep you from progressing, hold you in place, and reinforce the familiar patterns that keep you from moving ahead. They present themselves as "opportunities," an opportunity to take the easy way out, stick with what you know, and avoid a difficult conversation. They strengthen the invisible walls of the box.

You can identify these moments by how they make you feel. They feed the parts of you that crave safety and predictability. They are the invitations to repeat the actions that keep you trapped in the unholy trinity of stagnation: indifference ("It doesn't really matter"), indecision ("I'll think about it later"), and procrastination ("I'll do it tomorrow"). Together, they're the soothing sound of the conveyor belt, holding you in place. An opportunity to stay in place is the choice to scroll social media for another thirty minutes instead of using that time for a morning walk. It's saying "yes" to a social outing you feel obligated to attend when you know you need that evening to recharge. It's remaining silent in a meeting, even though you have an idea, because it's easier than facing potential criticism.

Each time you embrace one of these moments, you cast a vote for staying the same. You strengthen the neural pathways of inaction. The danger is that these moments are insidious. They don't feel like failures; they feel like relief. But when you continuously embrace these small moments of stasis, they blind you to what you could become. Your world becomes an echo chamber of your own limitations. Breaking free requires you to become a vigilant observer of your choices, asking one simple question when faced with a decision: "Will this propel me forward, or will it hold me in place?" Your answer, in every moment, determines your future.

The Path Forward

Insight without action is a fleeting thought. Many people understand what they should do, but those who change their lives are the ones who develop the discipline to bridge the gap between knowing and doing. The path forward is not paved with good intentions; it is built, brick by brick, through your daily, consistent actions.

A preparation mindset powers this commitment. This is not just a positive attitude; it is an operational strategy, an equation for building unstoppable momentum:

Faith x (Self-confidence + Persistence + Continuous Learning)

Think of this as the physics of personal growth. The three active ingredients, Self-confidence, Persistence, and Continuous Learning, are powerful forces on their own. But without the multiplying force of **Faith**, their sum is zero. Faith is the foundational belief that a better future is possible and that you are worthy of it. It is the catalyst that activates the other elements. You can have all the skills and grit in the world, but if you do not fundamentally believe in your own potential and the value of your vision, you will never truly commit to the journey. Faith is the strategic bet you place on yourself. It is the courageous act of saying, "I will build a way forward, even without a guarantee."

This faith is then multiplied by the active ingredients. **Self-confidence** is the quiet trust you forge in yourself by keeping the promises you make to yourself. It is not arrogance; it is the internal record of your reliability. Every time you do what you said you would do, no matter how small, you make a deposit in this account. This becomes the internal capital you draw upon to take calculated risks and step outside your comfort zone. **Persistence** is the operational grit required to navigate the ambiguity of the new economy. The conveyor belt offered a clear path; the path forward is one you must forge. Persistence is the engine of that forging process. It is the discipline to show up when motivation is absent and the resilience to get back up after being knocked down. It is the understanding that momentum is built not in giant leaps but in small, relentless steps. Finally, **Continuous Learning** is the adaptive engine for the AI age. The box rewards static knowledge; the open world rewards dynamic learning. This is the humility to know that your current skillset is not a destination but a starting point. It is the relentless drive to seek out new knowledge, challenge your assumptions, and see every setback as a data point for improvement.

These elements are not separate; they are a virtuous cycle. The more you learn, the more competent you become. The more competent you become, the more your self-confidence grows. The more confident you are, the more willing you are to persist through challenges. And the more you continue, the more you prove to yourself that your initial faith was justified. This is not just a formula for success; it is the operating system for anyone who has chosen to step off the conveyor belt and build their way forward.

This is your guide to implementing that equation. Five powerful habits will help you build momentum and turn understanding into action.

1. Reframe the Feeling of Relief

Choices that keep you stuck often feel like "relief." To break free, you need to consciously rewire this emotional connection. The next time you opt for comfort over courage and experience that wave of relief, pause. Reframe the feeling in your mind. Tell yourself, "This isn't relief." This is the feeling of stagnation. This is the cost of my future growth." By changing the name of the emotion, you interrupt the positive feedback loop that encourages avoidance.

2. Identify Your Anchor Habits

These are your specific, recurring behaviors that consistently keep you stuck. Take ten minutes and be brutally honest: what are your top three "anchor habits"? Is it scrolling social media before you even get out of bed? Complaining about a problem instead of exploring one small solution? Saying, yes to every social invitation out of a fear of missing out? Write them down. Then, for one week, focus on replacing just one of these with a more positive alternative. Naming your anchors strips them of their unconscious power.

3. Ask "What Would the Person I Want to Be Do?"

This habit links your daily decisions to your future self. When you face a choice, pause. Imagine the version of yourself you're working to become. Ask, "What choice would that person make right now?" The answer is usually quick and obvious. This shifts your decision-making from who you are now (with all your current fears) to who you want to become.

4. Schedule a Curiosity Hour

The conveyor belt rewards specialization, but a fulfilling life rewards broad curiosity. Block off one non-negotiable hour on your calendar each week for this purpose. This is your "Curiosity Hour." During this time, you must learn about something completely unrelated to your daily tasks. Read articles, watch a documentary, or explore an online tutorial on a topic you know nothing about. This habit prevents your world from becoming an echo chamber and is a direct investment in your future creativity and adaptability.

5. End Your Day with the "Propel & Place" Journal

The question, "Will this propel me forward, or will it hold me in place?" is most powerful when used for reflection. Before you go to sleep, take two minutes. Open a notebook and create two columns: "Propelled" and "Placed." Under "Propelled," write one choice you made today that moved you forward. Under "Placed," write one choice that held you in place. There is no judgment, only observation. This simple act makes you a vigilant observer of your own life, reinforcing your positive choices and bringing a non-judgmental awareness to the habits of stasis.

These five habits are your tools for liberation. They serve as manual overrides for the conveyor belt. Remaining on that belt is like outsourcing your future. Choosing to practice these habits is a brave act of taking control. Remember why this is so important: the invisible walls of the classroom and the corporate ladder weren't built for your benefit. They were designed to serve and advance the system itself, creating a predictable, manageable, and efficient workforce.

The system's goal is its own preservation and growth. Your goal must be your own. Remaining on the conveyor belt is like outsourcing your future; it limits your potential to a job description, and your fulfillment is measured by a fixed pay scale. It's a silent surrender. Selecting to move forward and practice these habits intentionally is a courageous act of taking control. Every time you rewrite your relief, question your anchors, consult your future self, feed your curiosity, and reflect on your day, you cast a vote. You are declaring that your life will not be a passive reaction to a pre-made system but a deliberate creation in your own design. The path ahead is not something you find, but something you build, one empowering choice at a time.

Section Two

Define Phase: Creating Your Vision for Success

Chapter 5

Your New Title: "The Architect"

We have explored the foundations of a world that no longer lasts. You have seen the invisible walls of the box, traced the conveyor belt's path, and realized that systems built for a previous era can't carry you to a future of your own making. This profound and unsettling truth marks the start of your freedom. You've done the brave work of looking beyond the illusion of safety to face the truth: the corporate ladder is unsteady, and the prescribed path often leads to an empty destination. More importantly, you have begun the essential inner work. You have confronted the whispers of uncertainty and self-doubt, choosing to arm yourself with the antidote of faith. You've committed to a preparation mindset, knowing that growth comes from consistent, daily effort, not luck. You have learned to show up for yourself, quiet the outside voices, and start searching for your own truth. Essentially, you have cleared the ground.

You have removed the debris of outdated expectations and broken ground on a new project: your life. But freedom is not a destination; it is a construction site. Escaping the box is the first act. The second, and far more critical act, is deciding what to build in the space you have cleared. To wander in this newfound freedom is to trade one form of passivity for another. It is no longer enough to criticize the old system; you must become the creator of a new one, a system of your own design, built on your own terms, for your own purpose. This requires more than a change in strategy. It requires a fundamental shift in your identity. It is time to graduate from the student, employee, or passenger role. It is time to claim your true title, which has been waiting for you all along.

That title is Architect.

This isn't a metaphor; it's a job description. It's the most important role you'll ever have. Why, you ask? Because you, my friend, are the architect of your life. For too long, you may have lived in a structure built by others your family, your educators, society's expectations. You've followed their blueprints, walked their hallways, and looked out their windows. Stepping off the conveyor belt means firing the pre-selected architect and taking your place, wielding the power and accepting the responsibility for yourself. You're declaring that you're in control.

Like any master architect, your work unfolds in three continuous phases: **Define, Design, and Build.** Embracing this process is how you turn the abstract desire for a better life into a tangible reality.

1. Define: Creating a Clear Vision

An architect never breaks ground without a clear vision for the structure's purpose. They don't just build "a building"; they build a home for a family, a hospital to heal the sick, or a museum to inspire the public. The vision dictates every subsequent decision. For you, the "Define" phase creates a crystal-clear vision for your life. This goes beyond vague goals like "be successful." It requires you to answer the deep, foundational questions: What does a truly fulfilling life look like for you? What values will serve as the non-negotiable pillars of your existence? What impact do you want your work to have? This is the soul-searching that gives your journey its "why." Without a powerful "why," the "how" becomes unbearable when challenges arise. Defining your vision is creating your North Star, the fixed point in the sky that will guide you through the fog.

2. Design: Creating Your Blueprint

Once the vision is defined, the architect creates a blueprint. The blueprint is the master plan, the detailed map that translates the grand vision into actionable steps. It is the bridge between where you are today and where you want to be. For you, designing your blueprint means getting tactical. It involves an honest self-assessment of your current reality, your skills, resources, habits, and network. With "here" established, you can map out "there." What skills must you acquire? What knowledge gaps must you fill? What relationships must you cultivate? Your blueprint is a living document, not a rigid plan set in stone. It is a strategic framework that outlines the projects to undertake, the people to learn from, and the personal evolution required to become the person capable of achieving the vision. It turns your dream into a project plan.

3. Build: Bringing Your Vision to Life

A beautiful blueprint is worthless if no one picks up a hammer. The "Build" phase is where the vision meets reality. It is the daily, consistent, and often unglamorous work of execution. This is where the preparation mindset, faith, self-confidence, persistence, and continuous learning becomes your daily practice. Building is deploying the tools, systems, and actions required to progress. A "tool" might be a new software you need to learn. A "system" might be a new weekly planning routine. And "actions" are the daily choices the "reps" you take to move forward. This is the phase where you will face the most resistance, but also where you build real self-confidence. Confidence is not a thought; it is a result, the byproduct of seeing yourself show up and do the work, one brick at a time.

This framework, Define, Design, Build, is your operational process. But before using it effectively, you must prepare yourself for the journey. The following sections are dedicated to this crucial preparation. We will explore how to reclaim the creative confidence you were born with and, most importantly, how to find the strength to start exactly where you are. This is the inner work that fuels the outer results.

Getting to Where You've Never Been

The poem *Invictus* closes with a powerful declaration: "I am the master of my fate, I am the captain of my soul." When you strip away the noise, this is the root of what our lives become. Your fate rests in your hands. Be empowered by that thought, not fearful of it. We are all trying to reach somewhere in life that we've never been before, a destination that pulls on our spirit of ambition and purpose. There is a gap between where you are and where you want to be. This is the core of Finding The Next You.

For every next step you desire, an evolution must occur. It is not about reinventing yourself but investing in yourself to become who your vision demands. For a freshman starting college, there is a gap between your first year and your last. The person you are as a freshman is not the person you must be as a senior to graduate as a young professional equipped to step forward in your career journey. Whatever path you choose, the gap between where you are now and where you want to be will always exist.

To help you navigate these changes and claim your new title I've created an assessment to measure your readiness to elevate to the next level. Remember, Finding The Next You is about investing in yourself to become who your vision for success demands you evolve into. You can find this tool in the Architect's Hub your digital design studio at FindingTheNextYou.com/assess. In just two minutes, you'll complete 20 questions and receive a customized report outlining your strengths and opportunities for improvement.

To close the gap, you must first assess your starting point. This begins with identifying your voice and vision for success. But before you can build a clear vision for "there," you must get brutally honest about "here." Think of yourself as the captain of a ship. A captain would never leave port without a detailed inventory of the ship's condition, fuel in the tank, the hull's integrity, and the crew's training. To set sail without this information would be reckless.

Similarly, your personal inventory is more than your current job title. It's a holistic look at your entire operating system. It means taking stock of your power skills: How effectively do you communicate? How resilient are you? How well do you collaborate? It means identifying your "anchor habits," like procrastination or negative self-talk. It requires acknowledging your limiting beliefs the stories you tell yourself about what you can and cannot do. This self-assessment is not an act of judgment; it is an act of strategic planning.

Once you have a clear picture of "here," you can define "there." Your destination needs to be so vivid that it pulls you forward. "Finding The Next You" means defining that next version of you with incredible detail. What does that person's daily life look like? What impact are they making? What values guide their decisions? A vague goal like "I want a better job" has no gravitational pull. A clear vision like "I will be a project leader known for inspiring teams and delivering innovative solutions" is a destination. It's a lighthouse in the fog.

The space between your honest assessment of "here" and your vivid vision of "there" *is* the gap. Please do not see it as a void or a sign of inadequacy. See it for what it is: your personal development arena. It is the space where the work gets done. The journey to Finding The Next You is a continuous cycle of assessing your current position, clarifying your destination, and doing the evolutionary work in the space between. You are the master of your fate. This is how you take the helm.

Finding Your Voice and Vision for Success

Finding your voice is a critical part of Finding The Next You. As we discussed earlier, most of us adopt the voice of others in the school system, our parents encouraging a "good job," society telling us which fields are hiring. Amidst all this direction, you may never have discovered your own voice.

During my speaking engagements, I have met countless young professionals who share the pain of living a life and pursuing a career they feel was forced upon them. They realize their voice and vision did not shape their life, but the pressure to obtain a specific degree or follow a predetermined path. Or their stories mirror mine: on the conveyor belt, following instructions, only to wake up one day feeling there is more to life. What overwhelmed me with uncertainty was the realization that I had not yet found my voice and vision for success. I knew where I was in my career was not where I wanted to be.

So, what does it mean to find your voice and vision? How do you know you are on your own path? You have found it when you can answer this question: *Where do you want your life to go? And why do you want it to go there?*

As Zig Ziglar said, "If you aim at nothing, you'll hit it every time." When you answer that question, you are defining your target. It is not a matter of being right or curating the perfect answer, but a matter of focus, effort, and self-correction.

- **Focus:** The intention to lock in on what you want. It means being determined to eliminate all distractions. You are focused not on the opinion of others, but on your faith in yourself.

- **Effort:** The energy you produce daily through your mind, body, and spirit. Focus demands effort; effort is the force you must generate consistently.

- **Self-correction:** As you gain experience, you will recognize moments that require adjusting your aim. When you miss your mark and you will, don't be discouraged. Readjust, recalibrate, and shoot your shot again.

Vision isn't sporadic; it shouldn't be a moving target but rather a living, adaptable one. The key balance for the architect lies in unwavering dedication combined with smart flexibility. Your vision serves as your North Star, offering a steady and dependable guide for your journey. It shouldn't fluctuate with trends or moments of doubt. Constantly changing vision isn't truly a vision but a whim, providing no anchor, and a ship without an anchor is at the mercy of every current. You need to stay committed to your "why," but also recognize that your initial idea of "where" is a hypothesis, not a certainty. As you progress, gain experience, and learn, you'll develop new insights that help you move forward.

You will see your destination with greater clarity. Think of it like an astronomer. Their goal is to study a distant star. At first, with a small telescope, their view is blurry, a vague point of light. But as they upgrade to more powerful instruments, the star doesn't move, but their view of it becomes sharper, more detailed, and more nuanced. They see things they couldn't see before. Your growth is like your more powerful telescope. You must not fall so in love with your first, blurry image that you refuse to look through the better lens. The architect's job is to distinguish between reframe and retreat. Reframing means adjusting your course based on new insight; it is an upgrade to your vision, often making it bolder and more aligned with who you are becoming. Retreat involves changing your course out of fear; it is a downgrade, a compromise driven by the tempting relief of avoiding a challenge. Do not alter your vision because you face an obstacle. The challenges on your path are not signs that your destination is incorrect; they are tests that build the strength and courage you will need to reach it. They are part of the learning process. The person who gives up on their journey at the first sign of difficulty was never truly committed to the destination; they were simply interested in a smooth ride.

In my experience, people fall into two groups. The first understands immediately what they want to do and why. The second group struggles to answer and claims they simply do not know. If you are in the second group, remember: if you aim at nothing, you'll hit it every time. Even when you're not entirely clear, aim at something. For most, the struggle is not a lack of vision but a fear of judgment. This fear is a mindset we must replace with one of preparation. Self-belief is the key.

With that understanding, no matter how big or small you believe your vision is, own it. It is not their opinion about you that matters; it is your opinion of yourself. Finding your voice and vision is about taking a proactive approach to your growth. If you remain fearful of trying new things, you will always be waiting to be told what to do. If you do not develop a plan for your life, someone else will.

You Were Created to Create

Somewhere along the way, our creative confidence is either celebrated or diminished. The term "creativity" was once limited to the arts. Then, social media introduced digital creatives. If you're not good at drawing, singing, or creating content, you might not consider yourself creative. Many people see themselves through this narrow definition, which prevents them from unlocking their creative power.

This narrow view is a disempowering lie. Creativity is not an artistic skill but the fundamental human act of bringing something new into existence. It is the essence of problem-solving. The entrepreneur who designs a new business model is a creator. The project manager who devises a more efficient workflow is a creator. The student who connects an idea from a history class with a problem in their computer science course is a creator.

Whenever you organize chaos, solve a puzzle, or build a plan, you are in a state of creation. Your voice and vision for success are not things to be found like misplaced keys; they are creations of your own making. Determining your desired life path is the most meaningful creative endeavor you will ever pursue. You begin with a blank slate, your future, and shape it with your ambition, values, and unique perspective. This opportunity is not exclusive to a privileged few; it is your fundamental right.

Why do so many of us feel we aren't creative? Our creative confidence often suffers because of the conveyor-belt systems we grew up with. Focusing on standardized tests and only one correct answer, the educational system trains us to think that exploration is inefficient and failure is final. These conditions help us become great consumers of information but gradually weaken our ability for creation. We start to fear the blank page, the judgment that comes with a new idea, and the chance of being wrong.

To find the next you, you must intentionally rebuild this creative confidence. Give yourself permission to be a beginner again. Start small. Look for a minor point of friction in your daily life, an inefficient morning routine, a cluttered desktop. Then, give yourself ten minutes to brainstorm three unconventional solutions. Don't edit or judge the ideas. Just create options. This small exercise retrains your brain to see problems not as dead ends, but as invitations to create.

Your life is your ultimate creative endeavor. The journey to Finding The Next You is recognizing that you are, and always have been, a creator. You were not created to follow a blueprint someone else designed. You were created to be the architect of your own blueprint and builder of your life.

As you define where you want your life to go and why you want it to go there, embrace your creative confidence. There are no right or wrong answers. This is your life, and you are the architect of it. The starting point is defining what you want your blueprint to be, a reflection of your voice and vision. At the center of that vision is your creative confidence.

There are no limitations and no judgments. These two components define the strength of your creative confidence.

- **No limitations:** There are no boundaries to who you can become. Dream as big as possible when you envision where you want to go. Color outside the lines. The only limitations are those we place on ourselves, often from allowing outside voices to put boundaries on our thoughts.

- **No judgments:** Do not be influenced by the opinions of others. Some friends and family, especially parents, mean well but can unintentionally cast doubt on your vision. When you embrace your creative confidence, you are not looking for acceptance. You believe it because you created it. I have witnessed talented young professionals bypass their dreams because they feared how others would judge their decisions. Don't let that be you.

People often project their own fears and uncertainties onto others. Remember, if you don't create a vision for your life, someone or something else will. Leverage your creative confidence to define your success without limits or judgment. Not everyone aims to be a millionaire or a CEO, which is perfectly fine. Beauty is in the eye of the beholder. Don't let someone call ugly what you have defined as beautiful. Define your voice and vision confidently, understanding that not everyone will understand it. They don't need to. The only approval you require is your own.

Start Where You Are

More often than not, you have to start alone. You must be willing to go alone to manifest the life you envision. The journey from where you are to where your vision takes you can be overwhelming. It is normal not to want to do it alone. Facing the uncertainty of new environments without someone you trust requires courage. This is one of the main differences between those who achieve their dreams and those who give up.

You don't wait for people to believe in your vision and join you. You don't require others to approve of your design. As the architect of your life, you understand that you are the only one you can hold accountable for showing up. You don't wait for permission. You start where you are.

No matter how you define your vision, it calls you to go somewhere you've never been. This is where uncertainty and self-doubt arrive, introducing you to fear. Fear attempts to get you to focus on all the unknowns, the skills you don't have, the questions that create doubt. It works to keep you in the familiar spaces that have defined your life until now.

To be effective in Finding The Next You, you must be willing to create a new normal. The entrepreneur who takes an idea from concept to execution had to start somewhere. The non-profit leader who provides immeasurable value had to start somewhere. They were like you, at a crossroads, trying to figure out the first step and building the courage to pursue their dreams.

Let's be clear: starting where you are, often alone, is not a sign of weakness. It is the ultimate act of strength and self-belief. It is when you stop waiting for validation and start generating momentum. The desire to wait for a co-pilot or a cheering section is a remnant of the conveyor-belt mindset. But you have chosen to step off. You have chosen to be the architect. The architect's first move is not laying a brick with a crew but drawing the first line on a blank page.

This is where the preparation mindset becomes your most critical asset. When you start where you are, you must redefine what "support" looks like. It ceases to be something you seek externally and becomes something you build internally. Your faith is the belief in the blueprint only you can see. Your self-confidence is the trust you build in your own ability to hold the pencil steady. Your persistence is the resolve to keep tweaking your blueprint even when you get discouraged. And your commitment to continuous learning is the humility to know your first draft will not be perfect. This internal support structure is far more reliable than any external validation because it is built by you, for you.

The fear that holds most people back at this stage is the fear of doing the work in the dark. We live in a world that celebrates the final result. Rarely do we see the thousands of unseen hours that lead up to that moment. It's the late night you spend learning a new software instead of watching TV. It's the early morning when you use to plan out your week instead of hitting snooze. This is the solitary work. It's not glamorous. But it's the work that creates the foundation. Every successful person you admire has a massive reservoir of these unseen hours. They started where they were, with what they had, and they did the work when no one was watching.

Embracing solitude is how you build a resilient core. When you learn to depend on your own discipline and vision, you become immune to others' opinions. You stop seeking the crowd's approval because you've gained self-approval in the mirror. A powerful paradox unfolds: the more comfortable you are starting alone, the more you attract the right people. Your clarity of purpose becomes a guiding light. Collaborators, mentors, and true supporters aren't attracted to uncertainty; they're drawn to conviction and momentum. Having the courage to begin where you are ensures that when people join you, they become part of a mission already in motion, led by someone who knows exactly where they're headed.

Chapter 6

Building Your GPS to Success

After a long week, you and your friends decide to meet at a new spot. You get the address, type it into your map app, and the GPS calibrates. A voice gives you turn-by-turn directions. You are on your way. Your screen shows the distance, the travel time, and your ETA. You are ready to reach your destination. A GPS is an invaluable tool. It guides you to new places, warns you of unexpected obstacles, and offers alternate routes to avoid crashes or construction. In the world we live in, we rely on it daily.

You have now identified your success destination where you want your life to head and why. This is a significant initial step. However, unlike finding a new restaurant, there's no dedicated app to guide you. There are no set, step-by-step directions, and your path isn't already paved. It's an adventure you create as you go, embracing the unknown with curiosity and courage. Unexpected obstacles, like a sudden layoff, a personal crisis, or a global pandemic, won't alert you with a notification. The calming voice of a digital guide speaking through your phone won't tell you when to turn. On this journey, you'll need to chart your own course and develop your own navigation system from within.

So, what do you do if your journey doesn't come with a pre-programmed app? You build your own.

As the architect of your life, you are also the programmer of your own internal GPS. This is not a device you purchase; it is a system you develop. While a car's GPS relies on external satellites, your personal GPS syncs with your internal compass. It navigates you not through streets, but through decisions, challenges, and opportunities. It is a dynamic, living guidance system that becomes more intelligent with every mile you travel. And like any sophisticated technology, it has several core components that must be understood and maintained.

First, your GPS relies on satellites. A physical GPS determines its location by signals from at least three satellites orbiting the Earth. Similarly, your internal GPS guides your decisions based on your core values. Values like integrity, growth, service, or freedom act as your fixed points in the sky they don't move. When you face a tough choice, like a fork in the road where both paths seem appealing or equally risky, your internal GPS doesn't consult a map of public opinion or societal expectations; it pings your values. It asks: Which path best aligns with the person I am committed to becoming? A job offer with a high salary may seem like the right choice, but your internal GPS will alert you if it conflicts with your core values of work-life balance or ethical impact. Living in line with your values keeps you on course, ensuring the path you follow is truly yours, not one shaped by someone else.

Next, every GPS uses a powerful algorithm that processes information and calculates the best route. Your algorithm is the preparation mindset. It is the operating system that handles every challenge and decision. When you face an obstacle, rejection, a failed project, or a difficult conversation, the algorithm doesn't just see a roadblock; it runs a calculation based on the formula we established: Faith x (Self-confidence + Persistence + Continuous Learning). Your faith in the destination prevents the GPS from shutting down. Your self-confidence tells the system you have the ability to handle a detour. Your persistence is the processing power that keeps searching for new routes instead of giving up. And your commitment to continuous learning allows the system to download new information, lessons from mistakes, to make future calculations even more accurate. This mindset allows you to navigate the chaotic and unpredictable landscape of life with adaptability.

Finally, the most important feature of any GPS is its ability to say, "Recalculating..." when you take a wrong turn. Imagine if your map app yelled, "You failed! The trip is over! You are a terrible driver!" the moment you missed an exit. You would throw it out the window. Yet, this is exactly how we often treat ourselves. We see a mistake or setback as a final judgment on our journey. Your internal GPS needs a strong "recalculating" function. This is the skill of adaptability and self-compassion. When a project fails or you realize you've been heading in the wrong direction, your GPS shouldn't crash. It should just say, "Recalculating..." and start charting a new path from your current location, using the new data from your "mistake." This isn't failure; it's course correction. It's the system working exactly as it should. Building your own GPS means accepting that detours and recalculations are not flaws in the journey; they are the journey.

Where Are You?

Before any GPS can give you a single instruction, it needs to do something very important: find out exactly where it is. It sends out a signal, determines its coordinates, and then shows a bright blue dot on the map, confidently saying, "You are here." Without knowing this starting point, any directions would be meaningless. A route from an unknown spot is just a series of random turns. The same goes for your life's journey. Having a big, exciting vision is great, but without honestly assessing where you're starting from, it's not really a plan just a daydream.

Self-assessment is one of the most challenging and brave steps you will take as the architect of your life. It requires you to quiet the noise, set aside your ego, and honestly view your current reality. The conveyor-belt world conditions us to avoid this. We're taught to build résumés that only highlight our strengths and to present an image of constant success on social media. But an architect can't afford to overlook a crack in the foundation or a weak point in the structure. To create something new, you need to first understand the ground you're building on. This isn't an exercise in judgment or self-criticism. A GPS doesn't judge you for being in a less-than-ideal location; it simply provides the data to help you reach your destination. Your self-assessment is your data collection phase. Let's break down the key coordinates you need to identify.

Coordinate 1: Your Power Skills Inventory (Vehicle Diagnostics)

Your skills are the vehicle that will carry you on your journey. It's essential to go beyond simply listing them; you must assess their condition. Are you operating a high-performance machine, or is it struggling and in need of maintenance? Be precise. Rate your ability to communicate persuasively, lead a team through challenges, adapt to unexpected changes, and think critically to solve complex problems on a scale of 1 to 10. Don't focus solely on the "hard skills" that look impressive on paper; those are becoming the baseline. The true power lies in your Power Skills. Recognizing that a skill is at a 3 out of 10 isn't a failure; it's the beginning of a plan to improve it to a 7 or 8. Ignoring it is like heading on a cross-country trip with a flat tire, hoping it will fix itself.

Coordinate 2: Your Mindset & Beliefs (The Operating System)

Your mindset functions like the software controlling your internal GPS. It can be an advanced system that recognizes opportunities and finds innovative routes, or it can be an outdated, faulty program that freezes or leads you in circles. Where do you stand on this spectrum? Pay attention to your internal dialogue. Is it a supportive co-pilot saying, "We can figure this out," or a critical backseat driver saying, "You're not smart enough for this," or "What if you fail?" These voices are your limiting beliefs, bugs in your mental code that impose false limits, marking certain destinations as "off-limits." Recognizing these beliefs, like "I'm not a natural leader," "I'm not good with money," or "It's too late for me to change careers," is akin to diagnosing your system. You must identify and address these bugs before you can fix them. An honest evaluation is essential because a top-tier vehicle with a flawed operating system will never reach its destination.

Coordinate 3: Your Environment & Network (The Surrounding Terrain)

No journey happens in a vacuum. Your environment the people you spend time with, the content you consume, the culture of your workplace is the terrain you navigate every day. Is this terrain a smooth highway, or is it a rocky, uphill path? Take an inventory of the five people you spend the most time with. Are they pushing you forward or holding you back? Are your conversations full of possibility and growth, or gossip and complaints? Your network is your support system. A strong crew can help you refuel, navigate, and make repairs. A weak crew can drain your energy and puncture your tires. Likewise, what information are you feeding your GPS? Is your daily intake a diet of inspiring podcasts, educational books, and challenging ideas, or a stream of mindless entertainment? Your environment influences your journey. When you're in a space that slows down your progress, it can drain your energy just to stay steady. Recognizing where you are helps you see which environments are helping you move forward and which might be holding you back.

Coordinate 4: Your Resources (The Fuel Gauge)

Finally, you need to evaluate your resources: your time, energy, and money. These are the fuel for your journey. A big vision without the fuel to pursue it is just a dream. Where are these resources actually going? Don't guess; check the data. Review your calendar from the last month. How many hours did you spend on activities that move you forward versus those that hold you back? Track your energy levels for a week. Which activities drain you, and which ones boost you? Look at your bank statements. Does your spending reflect the priorities of the person you want to become, or does it align with habits you're trying to leave behind? It's not about having a lot of money; it's about being a conscious steward of what you have. Being honest about your fuel gauge shows whether you're ready for a long journey or if you need to find a way to refuel.

Answering "Where am I?" by assessing these four coordinates reveals your glowing blue dot on the map. This is the crucial moment; while it can be humbling for many, it should never be seen as a defeat. Instead, it marks the point when guessing stops and navigation begins. At this stage, you, the architect, obtain a clear, unfiltered view of the land where you'll craft your masterpiece.

Creating Your GPS: The Calibration Process

Understanding the four coordinates is the first step. Now, it's time to move from thought to action. It's time to collect your data and establish your official starting point. To guide you through this critical process, we have created the Personal GPS Calibration tool. This is where you, the architect, survey the land before you draw the first line of your blueprint.

Let's be straightforward: skipping this step is like starting a road trip without letting your GPS find your current location after entering your destination. The route it suggests could be confusing, and setting bold goals without honestly understanding your starting point can cause frustration. This calibration is your moment of truth. It turns vague feelings about your life into clear data points. This information is crucial because it helps you be strategic. It guides you to the most important skill to develop now, uncovers the limiting belief holding you back, shows environmental factors influencing your progress, and clarifies where your resources are actually spent. Doing this activity is the ultimate act of "showing up for yourself" a commitment to stop guessing and start building with the precision of a master architect.

The Personal GPS Calibration isn't a test you pass or fail. It functions as a diagnostic tool, with its results serving as the foundation for your personal action plan-the first draft of your blueprint. The true value lies not in the scores themselves, but in how you utilize them to guide your next steps. The activity is meant to provide a clear, actionable starting point for each of the four coordinates.

For Coordinate 1: Power Skills, this activity will help you identify the single skill that, if improved, would create the most significant positive ripple effect in your life. It's not about trying to improve everything at once; it's about focusing strategically. Your results will give you Priority #1 for your personal development. This is the first renovation project you will undertake. Instead of feeling overwhelmed by all the options, you will know the one thing you should do first. This is a direct investment in the "Continuous Learning" component of your preparation mindset.

For Coordinate 2: Mindset & Beliefs, this activity encourages you to externalize your inner dialogue. By jotting down your "Supportive Co-Pilot" and "Critical Backseat Driver" thoughts, you diminish the unconscious influence of negative patterns. This will produce a clear list of the faulty code that needs rewriting. The subsequent step, which we will explore, involves systematically confronting and replacing each limiting belief with an empowering one, effectively upgrading your GPS's operating system.

For Coordinate 3: Environment & Network, your results offer a vivid visual snapshot of the influences acting around you. A list filled mainly with '-' signs in your "Inner Circle Audit" serves as a strong trigger for change. It gives you the insights needed to intentionally decide whom to invest your time and energy in. Likewise, noticing a heavily 'junk food' 'Information Diet' makes it clear that you can't ignore the quality of what you feed your mind. Your results essentially become a call to deliberately shape and manage your environment.

Finally, for **Coordinate 4: Resources**, your audit will probably be the most revealing. We often craft narratives about how we spend our time and energy, yet data rarely lies. Your results will clearly identify the leaks in your fuel tank. You'll see, in black and white, the difference between your declared priorities and your actual actions. This isn't meant to induce guilt; instead, it's an opportunity for empowerment. Your data provides a clear goal: cut the "Energy Drainer" by 10% and redirect the hours spent on "Time-Waster." This approach helps you move from resource shortages to building a surplus that supports your vision.

Completing the GPS calibration worksheet is more than just a reflection; it acts as your initial set of turn-by-turn directions. It shows the true location of your "You Are Here" dot. Embrace the clarity it provides. When combined with your willingness to act on this data, it becomes a vital first step toward progress. Access the GPS tool now in the Architect design studio at, *FindingThe NextYou.com/gps*.

Getting Stuck on Start

You've done the work. You have wrestled with your vision, you've embraced your creative confidence, and you've completed the courageous act of pinpointing your "You Are Here" dot. You have the destination plugged into your internal GPS and a clear understanding of your starting coordinates. A wave of energy and motivation washes over you. You can see the future you want to build. You are ready. So why is the car still in park? This is the most dangerous and deceptive phase of any journey: the gap between inspiration and action. It is the place where countless dreams go to die. It is the great static of the starting line, and learning to overcome it is the true test of an architect.

The reason so many people get stuck at the start is because of a deeply ingrained myth promoted by the conveyor-belt world: the myth that success is either given or earned. Society teaches us a transactional model. If you get good grades, you earn the diploma. If you perform well at your job, you get the promotion. This fosters a passive mindset, a belief that if we wait long enough or are "good" enough, someone will eventually give us permission to move forward. We wait for the perfect timing, the right connection, or for someone to recognize our talent. But the truth known by the architect is: success is neither given nor earned. It is built.

True success, the kind that leads to fulfillment and purpose, is not a reward handed out by a system. Instead, it is a structure you build with your own hands, guided by a blueprint that is uniquely yours. This blueprint is born from your creative confidence-your innate ability to see a better reality and devise a plan to bring it into existence. It is rooted in your unique gifts, passions, and the problems you feel called to solve. The conveyor belt offers a one-size-fits-all instruction manual, but the architect creates a custom design. The only way to turn that design into reality is to start building.

This is where the abstract meets the concrete. Reality isn't just something you think or dream about; it's what you create with your mind, spirit, and, most importantly, your hands. It is the real outcome of action. The vision in your mind is a beautiful ghost until you shape it into reality. You shape it by making the sales call, writing the first line of code, sending the email, having the uncomfortable conversation, or laying the first, imperfect brick. This is the step most people fail to take. They get excited about their vision but are reluctant to do the mundane, unglamorous, and often difficult work of building.

Why does this transfer sometimes fail? Because motivation is a fleeting emotion, a spark. It's the feeling you get after watching an inspiring speech, listening to a podcast, or reading a powerful book. It's real, but it doesn't last long. Motivation alone can't sustain a life; it needs to be turned into sustained momentum. Momentum isn't just a feeling; it's a tangible force built through consistent effort. This is where the preparation mindset, your internal GPS's algorithm, becomes your operational plan. It's the system that turns the spark of motivation into consistent actions that build momentum.

Consider it this way: when you're stuck at the start, your faith in the blueprint is what helps you ignore critics and doubters. It's the unwavering belief in your goal, even when the path isn't clear. It's that internal "knowing" that pushes you forward when there's no external proof. Your self-confidence gives you the courage to pick up the hammer for the first time, even if you're clumsy or unsure. It's the trust you build in yourself through small wins like waking up on time or finishing a workout, which then gives you the confidence to face bigger challenges. It's that quiet, inner record of your dependability. Your persistence is what keeps you going back to the construction site every day, especially on days when motivation is low. It's understanding that a skyscraper is built one brick at a time, and your only job today is to lay the next brick carefully and perfectly, regardless of how you feel. Persistence is the remedy for the emotional ups and downs of a long-term project. Your dedication to continuous learning shows humility, knowing you will make mistakes. You'll lay some bricks crooked, tear down walls, and rebuild. But each mistake isn't a failure; it's a lesson in masonry. It's data that makes you a better builder. It's the architect's promise to keep improving with every action.

Countless people find inspiration. They define their vision and feel a surge of possibility. However, they stay stuck at the starting line because they wait for motivation to carry them all the way to the finish. They wait for perfect conditions, for their fear to fade, or for someone to give them a guarantee. The architect understands that such a guarantee does not exist. Architects don't wait for motivation; they create momentum. They understand a fundamental law of emotional physics: action doesn't come from motivation; motivation comes from action. The only way to feel like doing the work is to start doing it, even when you don't feel like it. The confidence you want is on the other side of the actions you're avoiding. They recognize that the only way to reach their success is to start the engine and keep moving forward, even if the first mile feels slow and tough. It's time to turn your vision into reality. It's time to start building.

The Knowing-Doing Gap

When you define your vision and identify your starting point, a realization occurs. You see the significant gap between the world you wake up to every day and the one you dream of. This is the Knowing-Doing Gap. It is the large, daunting space between who you are now and who you want to become. It's the distance between your plan and the actual structure. For many, this is the moment they get stuck at the start, which causes most dreams to quietly fade away. The size of this gap can feel overwhelming, and doubt whispers, "How can I possibly get from here to there?" I believe this won't be true for you because you will change how you see this gap.

Everyone has to start somewhere, and no one begins as a master in their industry or area of expertise. The CEO of a Fortune 500 company once started as an intern. The renowned author once stared at a blank page, terrified. The world-class athlete once took their first awkward steps. They all faced a gap between their ambition and their ability. The key is that they saw the gap not as a void to fear but as a training ground to enter. Think of the story of David. Before he was king, he was a shepherd boy. In the quiet solitude of the mountains, he wasn't just watching his father's sheep; he was closing his gap. Every time he fought off a lion or a bear, he was building the courage and skill that would one day allow him to face Goliath. Each challenge, faced outside of the spotlight, was a brick in building his future. He worked tirelessly in his gap.

We all have a gap, regardless of the size of our aspirations. Your gap might be the Power Skills you need to develop, the network you need to build, or the limiting beliefs you need to overcome. As you prepare to create and execute your blueprint, don't let the gap between your current state and the future you envision intimidate you. Instead, learn to see it as your personal construction site. It is the space where the "Next You" is built. It is your gym, classroom, and laboratory all in one. The existence of the gap isn't a sign that your vision is too big; it's proof that your vision is big enough to be worth pursuing. It's a sign that you're aiming for growth.

The conveyor-belt mindset teaches us to fear gaps. It encourages us to stay on a predictable path where each next step is always clear and easily accessible. But as an architect, you must become skilled at navigating the gap. You need to become comfortable in the space of "not yet." This is where the mindset of preparation becomes your daily habit. Your faith enables you to look across the gap and believe in your destination on the other side, even when the full path isn't visible. Your self-confidence gives you the courage to take the first step into the gap, trusting that you can handle the initial challenge. Your persistence keeps you moving through the gap day after day, especially when progress seems slow. And your commitment to continuous learning helps you build the bridge across the gap, gaining the knowledge and skills you need, one step at a time.

Don't let the gap stop you from beginning. You know your destination and where you stand right now. The space between isn't a barrier; it's part of the journey. Now is the time to focus on what's next and take that step forward.

Section Three

Design Phase: Creating Your Blueprint

Chapter 7

The Architect's Hub

Your Life Design Studio

In the previous section, we outlined the core mindsets of an architect: a commitment to self-confidence, persistence, and continuous learning. These are more than just positive attitudes; they form the internal structure that helps you navigate the uncertainties of designing your life. They serve as the psychological toolkit that enables you to overcome the inevitable obstacles ahead. When faced with a challenge, you might need to reflect on a mistake; your commitment to continuous learning will highlight the knowledge gap you need to address. Without this mindset, you might blame others or circumstances. With it, you take responsibility. An opportunity might call for you to step into unfamiliar territory; your self-confidence empowers you to move forward with curiosity instead of fear, helping you recognize the possibilities that this new space can offer.

Remember, success is not earned or given; it is built. As the architect of your life, you need both the right mindset and the right skillset to build your way forward.

Mindset is just one part of the equation; the other is your skillset, which we'll now examine. Your vision starts in your mind, but it needs to develop into a blueprint before being brought to life. Transitioning from idea to reality requires cultivating the skillset of a master builder. This goes beyond mere willpower; it involves a practical system of operations. To construct, you need **Tools.** In addition, you must establish **Systems**. Most critically, you must be adept at taking decisive **Actions**. Together, these mindsets and skillsets create your personal success framework.

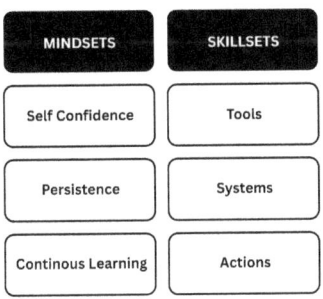

Life Architect Success Framework

As the architect of your life, what kind of structure do you want to build? The process begins internally: your mindset forms the invisible foundation deep beneath the surface, while your skillset constructs the visible framework that others will see. A weak foundation filled with self-doubt and inconsistency cannot support a grand design, regardless of how attractive the blueprint is. That's why our journey started with inner work. However, a foundation, no matter how solid, is pointless if it remains just a slab of concrete on an empty lot. You're not building for a moment; you're building for a lifetime. A temporary shelter can be assembled with cheap materials and amateur skills, but a true legacy of quality, durability, and character must be built with mastery.

You've already done incredible internal mindset work, now it's time to channel that growth externally by developing new skills. It's the shift from the drafting table, where you created your blueprint, to the construction site. Think of a master surgeon. Their success isn't just due to their calm demeanor and steady hands (their mindset); it also depends on their deep, practiced mastery of surgical instruments, procedural systems, and decisive actions in the operating room. One isn't effective without the other. This is the moment to commit to the same level of professional excellence for your most important project yet. Many people with great ideas and positive attitudes never achieve meaningful results because they fail to master their craft. They lack the practical operating system to turn their internal vision into external reality. To build the life you want, you need your own set of master tools and must become relentlessly skillful in using them.

But here is the challenge that stalls so many aspiring architects: *What type of life do I want to build and where do I start building it?*

To bridge the gap between the guidance of this book and the reality of your life, you need a dedicated workspace. You need an environment designed to foster focus, encourages self-belief, builds community, and provide the exact tools you need at the moment you need them.

This is why I created The Architect's Hub, your Digital Design Studio.

Imagine a space where the deafening noise of the world's expectations finally fades into silence. In this space, the pressure to conform evaporates, replaced by the freedom to create. This Studio is not merely a website or a resource library; it is a sanctuary for your ambition. It is the vast, light-filled room where you stand before the blank canvas of your future and curate, with creative confidence, a vivid mural of all your life's dreams.

In the outside world, dreams are often fragile things, easily crushed by cynicism or the crushing weight of "being realistic." But here, in your Studio, your dreams are protected. The Hub acts as your creative fortress a dedicated safe space where you can pin your wildest ambitions to the wall and stare at them without judgment. It is the place where you finally discover your true voice as the architect of your life, speaking clearly above the din of the conveyor belt.

But a Studio is not just a place to dream; it is a place to become. It is a training ground stocked with the tools, systems, and community that support your efforts to bring those dreams to life. Here, you are never building alone. You are surrounded by a community of fellow architects young professionals just like you who are also rolling up their sleeves to do the work.

By engaging with this ecosystem, you are doing more than just planning; you are evolving. You are developing into the builder your dreams require you to become, closing the gap between potential and reality one day at a time. This is the space where you forge the discipline and the courage to ensure that, one day soon, you will wake living in a life you once only saw in the dreams of your mind.

Throughout this chapter, as we explore Tools, Systems, and Actions, understand that you do not have to create these resources from scratch. I have stocked the Digital Design Studio with them. They are waiting for you, ready to be picked up. Enter your design studio now at: *FindingTheNextYou.com/start*

Tools: The Instruments of Creation

When discussing tools, we're not limited to physical objects. For the Life Architect, a tool encompasses any resource, framework, or knowledge that assists in turning your vision into a concrete plan and ultimately into action. Your mindsets represent the "why" behind your efforts, while your tools embody the "how." They are the instruments used to assess your initial position, draft your blueprint, and establish your foundation. These are the everyday tools you employ to shape your world.

The first and most important tool is your **Internal GPS**, which we covered in the last chapter. It is the master tool that allows you to define your destination and identify your "You Are Here" dot. But a GPS only tells you where you are and where you want to go. To navigate the journey, you need more specific instruments.

The Architect's Canvas, before an architect drafts a technical blueprint, they often create a concept board to capture the feeling of the project. This is your **Architect's Canvas**. It is a dynamic, visual workspace within the Hub where you can curate the mural of your life. This is where you pin the images that inspire you, the quotes that fuel your resilience, and the links to the videos and podcasts that are shaping your thinking. While your Blueprint appeals to your logic, your Canvas appeals to your emotion. It serves as your daily source of visual inspiration, reminding you not just *what* you are building, but *why* it is beautiful.

A **Daily Planner**, whether digital or paper, is a tool. It's more than a to-do list; it is the instrument you use to turn your long-term vision into specific, actionable tasks for the next 24 hours. A to-do list passively lists obligations; a planner actively states your priorities. It's the tool that lets you "pay yourself first" with your time, blocking out non-negotiable appointments with your future self before the world fills your schedule with its demands. It serves as the bridge between your quarterly goals and your next hour of focused work.

A Skill Development Plan is an essential tool. It's the framework you develop to deliberately address the knowledge gaps you identified in your GPS Calibration. It transforms the vague idea of "I need to get better at communication" into a specific plan: "This month, I will read one book on public speaking, watch two TED Talks on storytelling, and practice my next presentation in front of a mirror three times." This tool helps you avoid random acts of learning and instead concentrates your efforts on the exact skills your blueprint requires. It is your personal curriculum, designed by you, for you.

Other tools in your toolkit might include a personal budget, which helps you allocate your financial resources toward your goals, or a networking tracker, designed to help you intentionally build relationships that support your journey. You could also adopt a "Decision Journal," a simple notebook for recording important decisions, the reasoning behind them, and their outcomes. This tool enhances your judgment by creating a feedback loop, enabling you to learn from both successes and mistakes. Remember, a tool is only effective when you become skilled in using it. A master carpenter can craft a masterpiece with a basic chisel, while a novice can make a mess with the most advanced power tool. The carpenter's power isn't in the tool itself but in the thousands of hours of practice that make the tool an extension of the user's skill.

Your job as an architect is not just to collect a box of shiny, unused tools, but to select a few vital ones and commit to mastering them. Practice using your planner every single day until it feels unnatural to start your morning without it. Refer to your Skill Development Plan weekly until it becomes the default filter for the content you consume. Your tools are what allow you to move from dreaming to doing. They provide the structure for your ambition and the mechanism for your focus. They are what give your hands the ability to build what your mind has envisioned.

Systems: The Foundation of Consistency

If tools are the instruments you use to build, systems are the foundational structures and consistent habits you implement that make the building process possible. A tool is what you use; a system is how you work. An architect knows that a skyscraper is not built in a single burst of inspiration. It is built through the relentless, day-in, day-out execution of a proven process. Systems are what ensure that progress happens even when motivation fades. They are the antidote to inconsistency. Willpower is a finite resource that gets depleted throughout the day. Systems are a strategy for conserving that willpower for the most important, high-stakes decisions, while automating the rest. They are your personal infrastructure for success.

Think of a modern skyscraper. The steel beams and glass are the tools and materials. They are what you see. But what makes the building a functional marvel are its interconnected operating systems: the electrical grid, the plumbing, and the HVAC system. Without these integrated systems working in harmony, the building is just a beautiful but lifeless shell. A failure in one system will inevitably cause damage to others. Similarly, a well-built life requires its own interconnected "Operating System."

In the Digital Design Studio, we don't just talk about systems; we operationalize them. The Hub is designed to be the "Operating System" for your life, integrating seven fundamental personal systems that, when working together, create the consistent habits that make your progress inevitable. This system consists of seven fundamental personal systems. Each manages a critical resource, and when they work together, they create the consistent habits that make your progress not just possible, but inevitable.

To consistently execute on your ideas, you will need to deploy the following seven systems.

1. System of Development: Your Personal Curriculum for Growth

This system formalizes your commitment to continuous learning. It provides a structured plan for developing new skills and knowledge. One of the keys to sustained success is adopting a growth mindset, and this system is how you live it out. It involves intentionally identifying the knowledge gaps from your GPS Calibration and actively seeking out books, courses, mentors, and experiences that will fill them. It's a system to ensure that the "you" of next year is more capable than the "you" of today. This isn't about passively consuming information; it's about actively acquiring and applying it. Your System of Development should include time for both learning and doing. For every hour you spend reading a book, you should schedule an hour to practice that new skill in a real-world, low-stakes environment. This system transforms you from a student who collects certificates into a practitioner who builds competence. It's the engine of your evolution.

2. System of Time: Mastering Your Most Valuable Asset

Your System of Time is how you turn your big vision into actions over the next 24 hours. This goes beyond just a to-do list. It's a system for prioritizing tasks based on your vision, setting aside time for deep work, and shielding your schedule from distractions. You need to become the master of your minutes because your minutes make up your life. A strong System of Time includes a weekly planning session where you identify your top priorities that match your blueprint. Then, you schedule these priorities into your calendar first before it fills up with others' agendas. This system treats your time as the valuable, limited resource it is. It helps you tell the difference between being "busy" and being "productive." Busyness means reacting to the urgent; productivity means acting on the important.

3. System of Preparation: Building Confidence Through Readiness

The success you want tomorrow depends on how you prepare today. Execution is not about luck; it's about the confidence built through thorough preparation. Your System of Preparation shows your commitment to doing the unseen work. This includes researching the company before the interview, practicing your presentation until it feels natural, and planning your week on Sunday night. This system helps you not only to seize opportunities but also to create them through your readiness. Preparation involves anticipating future needs and challenges and solving them beforehand. It's the habit of asking, "What could go wrong here, and how can I prevent it?" This system is what distinguishes amateurs from professionals. Amateurs practice until they get it right; professionals practice until they can't get it wrong.

4. System of Clarity and Creativity: Quieting the Noise

Our lives are full of distractions that seek to manipulate our emotions and trap us in fear. Your System of Clarity and Creativity is your defense. It's the daily practice through journaling, meditation, or quiet reflection that helps you quiet the noise and reconnect with your vision. With clarity, you can see obstacles not as barriers but as problems to solve. With creativity, you can transform those problems into fuel. This system is your dedicated space for strategic thinking. The busy world constantly keeps you occupied with tasks, leaving little time to think. An architect must create this time. A daily journaling practice, for example, is a system for untangling the thoughts in your head, identifying the root of anxieties, and brainstorming solutions.

5. System of Productivity: Your Engine for Momentum

This system provides the energy needed to achieve consistent results and guards you against two main obstacles: inconsistency and procrastination. Your Productivity System may include habits like the "Five-Minute Rule" to break inertia or a structured weekly review to monitor progress. If left unchecked, these obstacles can undermine your productive efforts. The system acts as your shield, helping you design your environment and workflow to make doing the right thing easier. This might involve turning off phone notifications during deep work or preparing healthy meals in advance. A well-designed productivity system doesn't depend solely on willpower; it minimizes the need for it.

6. System of Wealth: Your Plan for Financial Stewardship

Money should work for you, not make you a slave. Your System of Wealth is your plan for managing your finances wisely. It begins with the idea that how well you handle $1,000 shows how well you'll handle $100,000. This system involves making a budget, creating savings and investment plans, and learning about financial literacy. You don't need a lot of money to start building your vision, but you must manage what you have effectively to grow your impact. This system is about more than just paying bills; it's about using money as a tool to build your future. Financial stress is one of the biggest killers of dreams. A strong System of Wealth brings peace of mind and financial freedom, enabling you to take smart, calculated risks.

7. System of Wellness: Your Most Essential Vehicle

Your mind, spirit, and body function as your most vital system. This is the vehicle that drives you toward your destiny. Your System of Wellness is your non-negotiable commitment to maintaining and renewing this vehicle daily. It encompasses your habits around sleep, nutrition, exercise, and mental rest. Neglecting this system is like trying to build a skyscraper with a worn-out crew; eventually, everything stalls. This system is not a luxury; it is an essential strategic necessity. Your "mind" wellness includes your System of Clarity.

Your "spirit" wellness involves connecting with your purpose and values. And your "body" wellness concerns the physical energy needed for peak performance. This means scheduling your workouts with the same importance as a client meeting and prioritizing 7-8 hours of sleep as the ultimate productivity tool.

Actions: The Currency of Reality

Tools and systems are essential, but they are worthless without the final, most critical component of your skillset: **Actions.** Action is the currency of reality. It is the only thing that can turn a blueprint from paper into a physical structure. You may have the best tools and the most brilliant systems, but if you're not willing to take decisive action, you are not an architect; you're a dreamer. This is the key difference. A dreamer finds satisfaction in the elegance of the blueprint; their reward is the feeling of potential. An architect finds satisfaction in laying bricks; their reward is the feeling of progress. Dreaming is safe. Building is risky. The world is full of people with perfect, dust-covered blueprints for lives they never lived. The world was built by architects who took their imperfect plans into the field and had the courage to lay the first brick.

This courage is not a feeling; it is a choice. More accurately, it is a discipline. It is the **discipline of doing**. This is the core muscle every architect must develop. Motivation is a fair-weather friend; it appears when the sun is shining and the work is exciting but disappears at the first sign of trouble. Discipline, however, is the all-weather companion who shows up every single day, rain or shine, because it has committed to do so. The dreamer waits for motivation to strike before acting. The architect understands that only through action can that feeling be generated. Taking action is the essential bridge that helps you push past excuses, tiredness, and fear. It's a straightforward, humble, yet impactful decision to proceed with the work no matter what. This discipline isn't about forcing yourself into a joyless grind; rather, it's the practice that produces deep, earned satisfaction from seeing real progress on a project that matters to you. It is the foundation of true momentum.

The ability to take action is a skill fueled by self-confidence. Every time you make a decisive choice and act on it, you are voting for the person you want to become. This isn't about being reckless; it's about overcoming the paralysis of indecision. The architect knows that the world is built by those willing to make choices and move forward, even with incomplete information.

Taking action means picking up the hammer. It's sending the email you've been drafting in your head for a week. It's making the phone call you've been dreading. It's signing up for the course you've been considering. Action generates data. You will learn more from laying the first ten bricks than from ten hours of reading. This is where action fuels your commitment to continuous learning. Your actions generate outcomes, both positive and negative, which serve as feedback for refining your blueprint.

Ultimately, your success will be measured not by the brilliance of your vision but by the sum of your actions. It is the consistent, courageous, and decisive actions you take every single day that will close the gap between the life you have and the life you envision.

This is the greatest value of the Architect's Hub. In the Design Studio, you are surrounded by the evidence of being committed to action. You are part of a community of builders who are also working to bring their blueprints to life. When you see others engaging with the tools and running their systems, it fuels your own discipline. It serves as a reminder that consistent action is the bridge that helps you cross the gap created by your own excuses.

From Blueprint to Building Site

We've just outlined the essential parts of your Architect's Skillset: the Tools, the Systems, and the Actions. It's natural to feel a mix of excitement and maybe a little overwhelmed. Think of it as the feeling an architect gets when they stand in front of an empty lot, holding complex blueprints for a skyscraper. The size of the project can be intimidating, but it's also exciting. My goal isn't to give you a strict instruction manual, but to provide the guidance for you to design your own blueprint. We're learning the universal principles of good construction, but you're the one who will choose the style, materials, and ultimate purpose of the structure you build.

No one becomes a master carpenter or architect overnight. Mastery results from a long and often unglamorous apprenticeship, involving a commitment to learning the tools, practicing the systems, and taking action, day after day. This is your apprenticeship. The journey of Finding The Next You isn't a race; it's a patient, deliberate process of becoming a master craftsman of your own life. The daily, repetitive actions like reviewing your planner, documenting your thoughts in your journal, or reading for 30 minutes are the modern equivalent of an apprentice sanding wood. They seem small on their own, but over time, they build mastery.

Building a quality life takes patience and care. We tend to notice and quickly dismiss poorly made things around us, whether it's a wobbly chair, a glitchy app, or a badly tailored suit. Naturally, we expect and demand better. It's important to hold that same high standard for your own life, which is arguably the most important project you'll ever work on. When your life is pieced together from other people's expectations, societal pressures, or random choices, it can feel just like that shaky, drafty house, unstable and never quite feeling like home. It might look okay from the outside, but deep down, you'll feel the insecurity of a fragile foundation, built on the shifting sands of external approval.

A masterpiece, on the other hand, is crafted with intention, integrity, and the best materials we can find. It is genuine from the inside out. Think of the materials for your life as your mindsets and skillsets. Your mindsets are like high-tensile rebar, those unseen strengths that give you resilience during life's storms. They are the grid of your beliefs, your self-confidence, your persistence, and your faith, holding everything together even when external forces try to shake you. This rebar might be invisible to others, but it's what truly makes you strong. Your skillsets are like the high-quality concrete and steel, the parts of your life that others see and interact with. These include your communication skills, technical knowledge, and productivity systems. They shape your life's form, function, and tangible power. Remember, a structure made only of concrete and steel, without rebar, can be fragile and break under pressure. Conversely, a rebar-only framework without concrete is just a formless cage. True mastery comes from blending these two elements harmoniously.

Your building's integrity depends on aligning your actions with your core values, while your intention derives from a clear blueprint you create. These two elements are the twin pillars of a master builder, distinguishing a mere structure from a work of art. Intention guides the direction; integrity guarantees the quality of the process. In construction, a plumb line, a weight hanging from a string, uses gravity to establish true vertical. An architect who disregards it builds crooked walls, resulting in an unstable structure. Your values are your internal gravity, your personal plumb line, and every decision should align with them. This isn't just about major ethical choices; it's about the countless small compromises made daily: taking shortcuts, telling white lies to avoid conflict, prioritizing short-term gains over long-term relationships. Each is a crooked brick. Though small individually, they add up to a life out of alignment, feeling hollow and inauthentic. Living with integrity creates a life that feels solid and genuine because it is. Meanwhile, intention is like examining the blueprint before you start building. Without it, a project becomes a series of random actions without progress or direction. An unintentional life reacts to the loudest demand or the most urgent email. An intentional life, however, is a deliberate creation, where you are the cause, not the effect.

Consider this chapter your orientation at the building site. You have been issued your hard hat and safety briefing. You now understand the fundamental relationship between your internal Mindsets and external Skillsets. This is the physics of personal architecture. The upcoming sections will transition from this orientation into your active apprenticeship. We will move from the "what" to the "how," offering practical guidance for setting up your seven core systems and cultivating the consistency needed for decisive action. This is where you learn to not just read the blueprint, but to bring it to life. This is where you learn to swing the hammer. You have surveyed the land, drafted the plans, and gathered your materials. Your foundation is cured and ready. Now, enter the design studio, pick up your tools and get ready to build.

CHAPTER 8

CREATING YOUR BLUEPRINT

We have traveled a significant distance together. You have dismantled the illusion of "later," recognizing time as your most valuable, non-renewable resource for building a meaningful life. You have chosen the power of self-focus, creating a shield against the pull of external expectations. You have begun the journey inward, finding the faith to overcome the whispers of uncertainty and self-doubt, and committing to a mindset of preparation. You have seen the invisible walls of the conveyor belt's box not as an inescapable prison but as a challenge to conquer. Standing on the cleared ground of your potential, you have claimed the title of Architect and accessed your design studio. You have calibrated your internal GPS, honestly assessing your starting point, and now understand the physics of personal construction, the fusion of internal Mindsets and external Skillsets.

Now, we reach the drafting stage. All preparation, internal shifts, and strategic insights come together in this key step: creating the blueprint. This is when the idea becomes tangible. It's the point of no return, where the dreamer commits to becoming the builder. Think of the journey so far as preparing to build your dream home: you've secured financing (your commitment), chosen the location (your vision's direction), and surveyed the land (your GPS calibration). Now, you're sitting with the lead architect yourself to translate all those dreams, feelings, and requirements into detailed plans. A realtor asks questions to find an existing house that suits you; an architect asks questions to design a new home tailored for you. This chapter is that design session, where you shape your reclaimed creative confidence into a concrete form.

Your blueprint signifies your declaration of creative independence. It marks the moment you stop following a pre-designed life and start shaping your own. For years, others have given you blueprints such as a professor's syllabus, a manager's job description, and societal expectations. Now, it's time to set them all aside. Your blueprint is your blank canvas, and making the first line is an act of courage. It requires you to silence the inner critic that whispers about being "realistic," a term often used to disguise the fear of failure. You must also build a shield against the external pressures to create a smaller, safer, and more conventional structure that fits within their box. In this sacred space of creation, we leave behind the word "realistic." We focus not on past limitations but on the endless possibilities of your future. There are no bounds or judgments this is your life, and you hold the authority to design it.

This is where your mindsets and skillsets come together. The blueprint you're about to develop embodies your preparation mindset and the operational strategy that will steer your journey from now on.

It transforms the equation Faith x (Self-confidence + Persistence + Continuous Learning) from an abstract idea into a tangible plan. Your faith is invested in the vision statement and the 'Future Self' letter, embodying a belief in a future that has yet to materialize. Your self-confidence is reflected in the act of writing, a show of your capability and worthiness to shape your own path. This blueprint becomes the strategic plan that demands and nurtures your persistence, the 'why' that sustains you through inevitable challenges. The 'Materials Inventory' you create, including skills, knowledge, and relationships, forms the curriculum for your continuous learning. This isn't just an exercise; it's the architecture of your ambition. Your blueprint lives in the details, and the questions below will guide you in creating it.

Blueprint Design Process
Theme 1: Professional & Personal Identity

(These questions focus on the "who" and the "how" of your daily existence.)

- Who do you want to be in your career?
- What type of person do you want to become?
- How do you want to show up in your relationships?

Theme 2: Impact & Legacy

(These questions focus on the "why" behind your efforts and the lasting effect you want to have.)

- Who do you want to impact?

- When people who know you best describe you, what three words do you hope they use?

- What type of legacy do you want to build?

Theme 3: Resources & Lifestyle

(These questions focus on the tangible resources and experiences that will fuel your vision.)

- How much money do you want to make?

- What does freedom (of time, location, or finances) mean to you, and what would it allow you to do?

- What is one experience you want to have in the next five years that would represent a significant step toward the life you envision?

The Architect's Blueprint Design Session

You have answered the guiding questions and regained your creative confidence. You now possess the raw materials for your vision. It is time to move from reflection to design. The following activities are your drawing board, with the step-by-step process an architect uses to turn a grand vision into a workable plan. By the end of this session, you will have the first draft of your master plan. This is not a casual journaling exercise; it is a focused, strategic work session. It is the moment you switch from being the client who describes the dream to being the architect who makes it buildable. Before you begin, create the right environment for this work. Find a quiet hour where you will not be disturbed. Put your phone on silent and out of sight. Approach these activities with the same seriousness you would bring to the most important meeting of your career because it is.

This session transforms your "why" into its "how." The guiding questions provided the core of your vision, and these activities will give it structure. You are shifting from emotions and desires to focusing on organization and strategy. This can feel daunting. The blank page can feel like a void, and there can be a strong urge to continue thinking, researching, or more "preparing to prepare" can be immense. You must resist this temptation. The goal here is not to craft a perfect, unchangeable final document, but to get the initial draft on paper. A flawed plan is far more valuable than a perfect dream sitting only in your mind, as plans can be edited and improved, unlike dreams.

Embrace the mindset of a creator. Be bold in your vision and brutally honest in your self-assessment. The "Future Self" letter is your opportunity to dream without limits. The "Materials Inventory" is your chance to be ruthlessly practical about what it will take to achieve those dreams. One without the other is useless. A grand vision with no honest assessment of the needed materials is just a fantasy. A list of skills to learn with no inspiring vision to guide them is simply a chore. This session combines the two. It's where your boldest ambitions meet your most grounded reality. Treat it as such. Take a deep breath. Pick up your pen. Let's begin to draw. To help you create a lasting artifact, we have created an interactive Digital Design Studio. You can access it at ***FindingTheNextYou.com/Blueprint***. This tool will walk you through each of these four activities, allowing you to create and download your own personalized One-Page Blueprint. This is your design studio, a space for you to create with freedom and courage. There are no limitations or judgments. You can also utilize a personal notebook or blank piece of paper. Whatever you choose, remember to embrace your creative confidence.

Activity 1: The "My Future Self" Letter (Establishing the Vision)

Your first step is to connect with the emotional core of your vision. Your blueprint is a living representation of your vision of happiness and fulfillment. Therefore, a blueprint without a purpose, interconnected with your soul, is just a technical drawing. This letter is the soul of your design. Utilize the digital design studio or take a single sheet of paper and structure it as follows:

- **What to do:** Write a one-page letter from your future self, five years from today. This "Future Self" is living the life you are beginning to envision. In the letter, have them describe a "day in their life" in vivid detail. What time do they wake up? What does their morning routine look like? What kind of work are they doing? Who are they interacting with? Most importantly, how do they *feel* at the end of the day (e.g., energized, fulfilled, at peace, proud)? Finally, have them give your present self one crucial piece of advice.

Why it works: This exercise moves your vision from a list of abstract goals into an emotional reality. It forces you to think about the *feeling* and the lifestyle you are building, not just the accomplishments. The advice from your "Future Self" often reveals what you intuitively know is the most important principle to guide your construction.

Activity 2: The Three Pillars (Defining Your Foundation)

Every great structure is built on a solid foundation. Your pillars are the non-negotiable values that will support every decision you make.

- **What to do:** Review your "Future Self" letter. Underline the words and feelings that resonate most strongly. Based on these, identify the three most important core values present in that future life. These are your pillars. *Example: If your letter described freedom, deep family connections, and work that helps others, your pillars might be: 1. Autonomy, 2. Relationships, 3. Service.* Write your three pillars down and, for each one, write a single sentence that defines what it means to you. (e.g., Autonomy means having control over my time and creative projects)

Why it works: This activity distills your emotional vision into a set of clear, actionable principles. These three pillars become the primary filters for your internal GPS. When faced with a choice, you can ask, "Does this align with my pillars of Autonomy, Relationships, and Service?"

Activity 3: The Materials Inventory (Sourcing Your Supplies)

An architect must know the materials needed to bring a blueprint to life. This is your inventory of the skills, knowledge, and relationships you must acquire.

What to do: Create three lists based on your vision and pillars.

1. **Skills to Acquire:** What specific Power Skills and technical skills does your "Future Self" possess? (e.g., Mastery of public speaking, Expertise in project management software, Ability to negotiate effectively). List the top three.

2. **Knowledge to Gain:** What topics or industries do you need to learn more about? (e.g., Personal finance and investing, The future of AI in my industry, Psychology of leadership). List the top three.

3. **Relationships to Cultivate:** What kind of people are in your "Future Self's" inner circle? (e.g., A mentor in my field, A community of like-minded creators, A personal board of advisors). Describe the types of relationships you need to build.

Why it works: This exercise transforms the abstract gap into a concrete shopping list. It provides a clear curriculum for your "System of Development." You no longer have a vague goal to get better; you have a specific inventory of materials you need to source.

Activity 4: The One-Page Blueprint (Your Master Plan)

This is the culmination of your design session. You will now synthesize all the previous elements into a single, powerful, one-page document that will serve as your guide.

What to do: Utilize the digital design studio or take a single sheet of paper and structure it as follows:

- **Title:** My Blueprint for [Your Name]

- **Vision Statement (from Activity 1):** Write a one-sentence summary of the core feeling and purpose described in your "Future Self" letter.

- **The Three Pillars (from Activity 2):** List your three core values and their definitions.

- **Key Construction Projects (from Activity 3):** Under three headings Skills, Knowledge, and Relationships list the top items from your Materials Inventory.

- **First Brick (Your Immediate Action):** At the bottom, write down the single smallest action you can take in the next 24 hours to begin your build. (e.g., Schedule my first 'Curiosity Hour' to research personal finance podcasts.)

- **Why it works:** This final activity creates a tangible artifact. It is the master plan you can look at every day. It is complex enough to be meaningful but simple enough not to be overwhelming. It connects your grandest vision to your smallest, most immediate action. This is no longer just a dream in your head; it is a blueprint in your hands.

Living Your Blueprint

Completing these four activities marks an important milestone. You have done more than just brainstorm; you have engaged in the disciplined, rigorous work of architectural design. The One-Page Blueprint you hold in your hands is not just a piece of paper; it is a declaration. It is the physical expression of your vision, the strategic roadmap born from your creative confidence, and the tangible symbol of your commitment to yourself. Treat it accordingly. This document is now the most valuable strategic asset you have. It is the constitution for the life you are creating.

A blueprint, no matter how brilliant, serves no purpose if left unused in a drawer or forgotten in a computer folder. Its true value is realized only when it becomes an active part of your daily routine. You need to foster a strong emotional bond with this document, as it embodies the core of the life you're aiming to build and the future version of yourself you're working towards. This emotional connection acts as your fuel, providing the motivation needed to overcome the inevitable obstacles encountered during the process.

How do you forge this connection? Make it visible. Don't hide your blueprint away. Print it out and post it somewhere you'll see daily on your bathroom mirror, above your desk, or on your nightstand. Incorporate it into your Architect Hour. Your morning routine should start with reviewing your Vision Statement and your Three Pillars. Let them ground you in your "why" before the day's distractions take over. In the evening, review your progress against your Key Construction Projects. Did your actions today match your design? This daily practice turns the blueprint from a static document into a living guide.

Most importantly, align with the emotion behind your blueprint. Recall the "Future Self" letter? Remember the sense of purpose, peace, or energy you imagined. That feeling is your true goal. The blueprint serves as a map, but the feeling acts as a guiding compass. When the journey feels tough, doubt arises, or the distance between "here" and "there" seems vast, revisit that feeling. Reread your letter or imagine your future self briefly. This emotional connection is what sustains your persistence. It helps you remember why you are building these blocks, making sacrifices, and choosing the challenging path of creation over comfort. You're venturing into unfamiliar territory, designing a life unique to you. Your blueprint is your navigation tool in this new landscape. Use it daily to stay aligned with your destination and to motivate each step forward. What started as a thought is now your road to turning dreams into reality.

Models & Mentors

On January 26, 2020, the world received the heartbreaking news that Kobe Bryant, his daughter Gianna, and seven others were tragically killed in a helicopter crash. Retired for nearly four years, Bryant was headed for induction into the NBA Hall of Fame.

As a young player, Kobe was labeled the next Michael Jordan (MJ). Early on, you could see how Kobe was building his game after MJ's pattern. One of the revelations that Kobe's death produced was the special bond MJ and Kobe had. Jordan tearfully shared insights into their relationship at Kobe's memorial service. Jordan talked about how his irritation with Kobe's persistent calls and questions quickly turned into admiration. MJ fell in love with Kobe's inquisitiveness and drive to learn.

There is no question Kobe utilized Michael as a blueprint. After a game, Kobe would humbly ask Jordan about his legendary fadeaway jumper, intent on perfecting it himself. It was the start of a special relationship that would push Kobe to be his absolute best. Through Jordan's example, Kobe discovered his own success and became the model for the next generation that Jordan was for him.

As Kobe modeled MJ, whose success are you modeling? Who is pushing you to be your best?

As you develop your blueprint, it is crucial to understand the two primary ways others can guide you: through modeling and through mentorship. They are not the same, and recognizing the difference is essential to using both effectively.

Models: Your Architects from Afar

A model is someone who inspires you from afar. These are people you probably don't know personally, but whose work, career path, or lifestyle you greatly admire. You can learn from their example without ever meeting them. Michael Jordan was Kobe's first model. Kobe studied his every move by watching hours of game tape, analyzing MJ's blueprint to grasp the principles behind his greatness. This is a very powerful tool. You're not the first to dream of shaping your own success. There are people who have successfully created a similar plan and brought it to life. These trailblazers are your models.

This process of modeling is an active, not passive, effort. It is a research project where the subject is a person's life architecture. Think beyond simple imitation. If your model is a successful tech founder, don't just admire their product; break down their journey. Read their early interviews and observe how their messaging evolved. Study their failed projects the ones often removed from the official biography to understand their resilience and how they pivoted from setbacks. In this way, you are not just a fan; you are an architectural historian. You are searching for the underlying structural principles, not just surface-level aesthetics. The same applies across any field. If you admire a writer, don't just read their bestselling novel. Read their debut novel, their essays, and even their negative reviews. See how their voice grew stronger, how they handled criticism, and what themes they revisited repeatedly. This is how you learn the craft, not just the outcome.

Finding your models today's world is easier than ever, but it requires intentional effort. It's not about mindless scrolling; it's about deliberate study. You can "model" an entrepreneur by following them on LinkedIn and analyzing how they communicate their vision. To model a creative director, study their portfolio and watch their interviews on YouTube to understand their thinking process. The key is to shift from passive consumption to active learning of their strategies. Ask yourself: What are their daily routines? How do they respond to criticism? What core principles seem to guide their decisions? It's also wise to assemble a portfolio of models. No single person will embody every aspect of your vision. You might choose one for their business skills, another for their creative integrity, a third for their work-life balance, and a fourth for their philanthropic efforts. By combining diverse examples, you're not copying but synthesizing unique principles to shape your own approach. Modeling is proactive learning. I suggest identifying at least three models that, in different ways, embody the success you aim for.

Mentors: Your Guides in Proximity

A mentor, on the other hand, develops through a one-on-one relationship. A mentor is someone who not only lets you study their blueprint but also sits down with you to give feedback on yours. They offer firsthand experience and wisdom because they are invested in your journey. While a model shows the "what" of the finished structure, a mentor can show the "how" and the "why." They are like the seasoned architect who reviews your plans and says, "I see what you're trying to do here, but have you considered this other option? I tried something similar on a project ten years ago, and here's the mistake I made." That kind of personalized, contextual feedback is invaluable. It can save you years of trial and error.

Michael Jordan became Kobe's mentor. The relationship shifted from being just a model to one of mentorship when Kobe's persistent calls were answered, and MJ started sharing his personal insights. While anyone can have a role model, true mentorship is earned. It results from showing your drive so that someone who has already walked the path is willing to invest their most valuable resource, their time, in you. Most people approach this the wrong way. They look for a mentor to provide motivation or open doors for them. But real mentors aren't interested in giving handouts; they're looking to make smart investments. They want to see someone who has already begun building and who has shown a commitment to their own growth.

Most people don't realize that mentorship often results from effective modeling. By observing your role models and applying what you learn, you start to generate results that catch the eye of potential mentors. Mentors are drawn to momentum, not just potential. Potential is a dream; momentum is the tangible outcome of your discipline. Your dedication to modeling proves you're ready for mentorship. This means doing the work first. Don't ask a potential mentor a question you could have answered with a simple Google search. Engage with them by adding value, sharing their work with a thoughtful comment, offering a relevant insight on one of their posts, or becoming a helpful member of a community they lead. When you do make a request, be specific and respectful of their time. Instead of, "Will you be my mentor?" try, "I've been applying your framework on X, and I've achieved Y result. I'm facing a specific challenge with Z. Would you be open to a 15-minute call to share your perspective?" This shows you've already put in effort and are seeking targeted guidance, not a handout. That's how you earn their time and eventually, their trust.

Building Your Community of Success

I've learned the importance of seizing opportunities when they arrive. I've become less concerned with failure and more focused on what is possible when I believe in myself and intentionally connect with like-minded individuals. In an age where technical skills can be automated, your ability to cultivate genuine human connections is a powerful differentiator.

Throughout our journey, we all need guidance and support. No successful person has reached their goals without help along the way. Kobe is one example among many. He built strong relationships with coaches and training experts to create a community of success that enhanced his abilities.

The pace of life can cause many people to get stuck in routines that don't bring the fulfillment they want. That frustration often comes from lacking real connection. We live in a world that promises more connection than ever, but heavy social media use can actually increase feelings of loneliness. Scrolling through highlight reels creates the illusion of connection without the depth of genuine relationships. As you create your blueprint, it's important to step out of your comfort zone and build real-world relationships.

I encourage you to press pause on your current routine. Identify where you can create time and opportunity to cultivate relationships with other architects. It is critical to your success that you bond with others who help drive you to achieve your vision. Don't allow your routine to isolate you from the power of community. Navigating your journey alone does not make you more authentic; it simply increases the likelihood of missing vital insights gained through collaboration.

Estimating The Cost

Many people don't realize until it's too late that the cost of inaction far exceeds the cost of pursuing their dreams. Being able to clearly express what you want to achieve is how you define your blueprint. Everyone, including you, has to pay the price of building it. There's no way around it. The success you seek will cost you something. There are no discount codes or free deals. You can't cheat success.

Everybody wants to be successful until they realize what it will cost. This is the great filter. It's the point where the dreamers turn back, and the doers roll up their sleeves. When they see the commitment and sacrifice required, many give up. They love the idea of the finished skyscraper but aren't willing to spend years putting in the effort to build it. Understanding the commitment needed highlights the importance of finding your models and mentors. They have already traveled the paths you plan to take. Their experience will help you prepare for the costs involved in your journey. By studying their paths not just their highlight reels, but their documented struggles you can get a realistic estimate of the costs involved. You learn that the "overnight success" was ten years in the making. This isn't meant to discourage you; it's meant to empower you. An architect with an accurate cost estimate can create a realistic budget and a sustainable building schedule.

Every day, you must pay a price for the blueprint you desire to build. What you pay isn't always money. Your payment can also come in the form of time, comfort, ego, and relationships.

- **The Cost of Your Time:** This is the most basic cost. It involves saying "no" to the good so you can say "yes" to the great. It's swapping an hour of passive entertainment for an hour of active learning. Every hour you spend is a transaction. Are you investing in progress or temporary comfort?

- **The Cost of Your Relationships:** This is one of the most emotionally expensive costs. As you build your new habits, people in your old environment may be uncomfortable with your commitment to your growth and development. You may have to lovingly create distance from them to protect your energy and focus.

- **The Cost of Your Comfort:** This is a daily investment in creating new systems and learning new environments.

It's the resistance you experience when venturing into unfamiliar territory. It involves opting for the discipline of growing your capabilities rather than staying secure in what's familiar.

- **The Cost of Your Ego:** This is the investment you make to learn new skills. It involves embracing the humility of starting as a beginner. It's about being comfortable with feeling a little silly sometimes, asking questions that might seem 'stupid,' and accepting that you might fail in front of others, all as part of your learning journey.

It is important to realize that you won't pay all these costs at once. An architect doesn't pay for every window and brick on the first day. Doing so would be reckless. Similarly, you shouldn't try to cover every personal and professional expense immediately. That approach leads quickly to burnout. Many ambitious people burn out because they attempt to transform everything all at once. This is not a sustainable building strategy.

Building is a process, and the costs are spread across different phases. Early on, the main costs include your time and ego. This is a period of intense learning, of being a beginner. As you start to build upward, the cost to your comfort and relationships may become more significant. This is when you need to create new systems and possibly distance yourself from environments and relationships that no longer align with your vision. Each phase has its own unique amount of energy, focus, and sacrifice.

One significant advantage of having models and mentors is the direct guidance they offer. A good mentor can help you effectively manage your personal budget by providing wisdom such as, "Focus on mastering this one skill for the next six months. Don't worry about that other thing yet." They can help you understand that progress is a marathon, not a sprint. The essential part is to be aware of the costs involved, be ready to pay them when they come due, and stay unafraid of the necessary investment. Your blueprint is worth the effort.

Chapter 9

Rebuild Your Routine

Time is complex and multi-dimensional. We started this book by emphasizing the importance of recognizing your moment when it's time to change, seize opportunities, or leave your comfort zone for growth. As you progress from planning your blueprint to executing it, you need to master managing your time effectively. Time isn't merely a resource; it's the primary currency, exchanged in every moment of life and the foundation for all other forms of value.

Most people believe money is their most valuable asset. A good financial planner will tell you that the first step in building wealth is to pay yourself first. Before paying bills, buying groceries, or spending on anything else, you set aside a portion of your income for your future. You establish systems to automatically transfer money into your savings, 401(k), or investment accounts. You ensure you are the first to benefit from the value you've created through your paycheck. This principle isn't about hoarding money; it's a powerful act of self-respect. It shows that your future deserves your best resources, starting now.

Nothing is more frustrating than looking at your bank account a few days after payday and wondering where all your money went. You forgot the online sale, the weekend with friends, and the impromptu take-out dinners. You paid the store, the restaurant, and the club, but you never paid yourself. Now, you're scrambling to make it to the next payday with what's left. This is the costly lesson of failing to pay yourself first. Without a plan, you will always invest your hard-earned money in places that offer little to no return on your future. You become a transactional hub for everyone else's priorities, leaving nothing for yourself.

There is no doubt that money is a crucial tool for creating the life you desire. However, it is not your most valuable asset. Time is.

If you lose money, you can earn it back. You can recover from a bad investment. You can find a new job. But time is different. It is the great equalizer and the ultimate tyrant. Every person on this planet, from the billionaire CEO to the struggling artist, is given the same, non-negotiable 24 hours each day. You cannot borrow it, inherit it, or earn more of it. Once you lose it, mismanage it, or give it away, you can never get it back. It is the one asset that is absolutely finite. This truth is both terrifying and liberating. It is terrifying because it underscores the immense weight of every choice you make. Each tick of the clock is a moment spent on either construction or decay, a vote cast for your future self or against them. A wasted hour is not just a lost opportunity; it is a permanent deficit, a piece of your life's potential that is gone forever. This realization can be paralyzing. It can breed a fear of commitment, a hesitation to act, because the finality of a wrong choice feels too heavy to bear. The weight of this truth is what keeps many people glued to the conveyor belt, preferring the known, predictable path because it absolves them of the terrifying responsibility of choosing. They trade their freedom for the illusion of a mistake-free journey, not realizing that the greatest mismanagement of time is to cede control of it to someone else.

Yet, this same truth is deeply liberating. It frees you because it shows that the ultimate game of life isn't based on the resources you're given, but on how you manage the one resource everyone has equally. It is the ultimate equalizer. The circumstances of your birth, your current financial situation, your network none of these can give you an extra hour in your day. This means that the person who learns to manage their time can outperform someone with every other advantage. It strips away every excuse. Your progress is no longer about privilege; it's about what you prioritize. This is the true source of the architect's power. You start with the same raw material as every other builder, and the quality of your final structure directly reflects your skill, discipline, and intention. This truth doesn't just invite you to take control; it demands it. It turns your daily tasks into a blueprint for your legacy.

With this understanding, you must apply the "pay yourself first" principle to your time with even greater discipline than you do to your money. Just as you create financial systems to invest in your future wealth, you must now build systems to invest your time in your future self. This is not a suggestion; it is a requirement for any aspiring architect. To pay yourself first with time is to make a sacred, non-negotiable withdrawal from your daily 24-hour deposit and invest it directly into your blueprint before anyone or anything else has a chance to claim it. Most people live in a state of "temporal debt." Their day begins, and immediately, withdrawals are made by others: the urgent email from the boss, friends calling with their drama, the notification from social media, the demands of family. By the end of the day, they have nothing left for themselves and are left with the hollow feeling of having been busy but not productive. They have paid everyone else first. The architect, however, reverses this flow. You make the first and most important investment in your own growth. This single act is the foundation of a proactive, intentional life. It is the difference between being the architect of your day and being a pawn in someone else's. As you prepare to transition from the design phase to the build phase, this is the most critical system you will implement.

The Time Audit: Where Does Your Time Actually Go?

Before creating a new budget for your time, you need to understand your current spending habits. Many people operate under the illusion of being busy. Our modern world excels at fostering this illusion. The constant stream of emails, endless notifications, and the pressure to be always on all contribute to a frantic sense of motion. We hurry from one task to another, our days packed with activity, and then collapse at the end, exhausted and feeling like we've worked hard.

But here is the dangerous trap, best summarized by the legendary coach John Wooden: "Don't mistake activity for achievement." Busyness is activity. Building is an achievement. Motion is not the same as progress. Just because you are tired does not mean you are any closer to your destination. The architect must become a master at discerning the difference. This requires a deeper understanding of the nuance of how we waste time, because the most dangerous time-wasters are disguised as productive work. The first thief is Reactive Work. This is the endless cycle of responding to what is loudest: the email notification, the chat message, the urgent request from a colleague. This work feels productive because you are active and checking things off a list. But in reality, you are playing defense. You are a goalie, blocking shots but never moving the ball down the field. Your entire day is dictated by other people's priorities, leaving no time to advance your own.

The second, more subtle thief is Shallow Work. These are low-impact tasks that require little mental effort but give a quick, satisfying sense of accomplishment. It includes organizing your inbox, endlessly tweaking the font on a presentation, or doing "just one more" search on a topic you already know well enough to start. This is a refined form of procrastination. You are working, but you are avoiding the difficult, deep work that truly leads to a breakthrough. It's like an architect spending all day sharpening pencils and cleaning their drafting table instead of drawing the plans. The activity is related to achievement, but it is not the achievement itself.

The illusion of busyness tricks you into feeling productive, but you're really just spinning your wheels. It's like being a hamster on a wheel, running furiously but going nowhere. You answer emails that don't align with your core goals (Reactive Work), attend meetings that could have been an email (Shallow Work), and scroll through social media in the name of "staying connected" (Distraction). These activities make you feel busy, but they are the very thieves stealing the time you need to invest in your blueprint. Reclaiming this time is the architect's main challenge. It takes the courage to leave a non-essential email unanswered for a few hours. It requires the discipline to close the social media tab. Most importantly, it demands the clarity of your blueprint to distinguish between activities that sustain your current position and achievements that shape your future. To break free, you must do what most people refuse to do: look at the data.

Life pays you with time, and its payroll schedule is daily. Every morning you wake, life makes a direct deposit of 24 hours into your account. Unlike money, this balance doesn't carry over. At midnight, any unspent time is gone forever. Each day, you choose how to spend this currency. To help you move from understanding that time is valuable to actually acting as if it is, we want to conduct a one-week time audit.

The purpose of this exercise is not to judge yourself. The goal is to collect data. An architect cannot design a renovation without first studying the existing structure. This tool is your survey. For the next seven days, you will be a neutral observer of your own life, tracking your "time transactions." You can track your time manually in a notebook, but calculating the hours can be tedious. To automate the math, you can use the digital Time Audit tool in the design studio at ***FindingTheNextYou.com/Time***. It will give you a data-driven report of your habits at the end of the week this data will be the catalyst for the intentional system you are about to build.

Designing Your "Pay Yourself First" Schedule

Starting your day without a plan means the day controls you; you don't control it. This is the default state for most of the world. To be planless is to be passive, like a ship without a rudder, at the mercy of the winds and currents. A day without a plan is driven by the loudest noise, the most recent notification, or the most urgent-seeming (but rarely important) demand. You are not the driver; you are a passenger being shuttled from one distraction to another. You are giving the day permission to spend your most valuable resource however it sees fit. It's like handing your debit card and PIN to strangers and hoping they make wise investments with it. They won't. They'll spend your currency on their priorities, dramas, and agendas. To build your blueprint, you must fire the crowd and become the sole financial planner of your time. You need to become the master of your agenda. The day must become your ally, not your enemy.

You're now shifting from observing to designing using the data from your time audit. You've identified how you currently spend your time; now, you'll create the ideal schedule. Remember, a schedule is just a framework; it's an empty grid, like a to-do list on a napkin. To make it effective, you need a solid system and guiding principles that shape how you fill that grid. The key is the unwavering commitment to paying yourself first. The framework below serves as your manual for this system. It helps you move from a defensive stance, protecting your time, to an offensive one, actively investing in your future. This is your path to winning the day every day.

Step #1 - The Architect Hour: Bookending Your Day

The most crucial change you can make is to claim the moments at the very beginning and very end of your day. We will call this The Architect Hour. This isn't about adding more work to your life; it's about making the work you already do more effective. It's the strategic pause that separates the professional from the amateur. An amateur builder arrives at the construction site and immediately starts swinging a hammer, hoping their activity leads to progress. A professional architect, however, understands that the most important work happens before the first nail is driven and after the last one is set. They know that an hour of focused planning can save ten hours of wasted labor. The Architect Hour provides these strategic bookends to your day, ensuring that your energy isn't just spent but invested. It's your commitment to working on your life, not just in it. This practice transforms you from a laborer, paid for your time, into an architect who creates value through vision and strategy. By claiming these bookends, you take control of your day's narrative. You're no longer reacting to the day's events; you're directing them. This is the ultimate power move, the first and most vital deposit you make into your future.

- **The Morning Routine (30 Minutes) - Your Daily Investment Plan:** Think of your morning routine as your daily investment planning session. A savvy investor doesn't start their day by randomly buying stocks. Similarly, you will no longer start your day by giving your time to the first email, text message, or phone call that screams for your attention. This is your moment to strategically decide where you will allocate your 24 hours to generate the highest return toward your blueprint.

    1. **Focus on Your Destination:** Spend two minutes rereading your "Future Self" letter or your one-page blueprint. Remind yourself *why* you are building.

    2. **Review Your Roadmap:** Briefly review your high-level goals for the week. What is the most important milestone you are working toward?

    3. **Define Your "Primary Investment":** Based on your destination and roadmap, ask: "What is the one action I can take today that will yield the highest return?" Identify that single critical task. This is your non-negotiable, "blue-chip" investment for the day.

- **The Evening Routine (30 Minutes) - Your Daily ROI Review:** Think of your evening routine as your daily portfolio review. This is your opportunity to assess the Return on Investment (ROI) of your day's efforts, celebrate your wins, and learn from your losses.

1. **Reflect:** How did your investments perform? Did you allocate your time and energy to your "Primary Investment"? What was the return? What went well? What unexpected challenges did you face?

2. **Reset:** Let go of any losses. If you made a poor time investment, acknowledge the data without emotion and move on. Every day is a new opportunity.

3. **Refocus:** Take the lessons learned. What is one insight you can apply to improve your investment strategy for tomorrow?

4. **Relaunch:** Prepare for the next day. Based on your reflection, define your "Primary Investment" for tomorrow. This will clear your mind and ensure you wake up with a pre-built plan, ready to win the day.

Step #2 - Time Blocking: Scheduling Your Deposits

Your Architect Hour sets the strategy. Now, you need a system to ensure that the strategy is executed. A to-do list is not enough. A list of tasks without a plan for when and where to do them is just a wish list, a collection of good intentions with no claim on reality. The most effective system for turning your intentions into action is Time Blocking. This is the practice of scheduling your day into specific blocks of time dedicated to particular tasks or types of work. Instead of just knowing what you need to do, you will now decide exactly when you are going to do it. This simple change distinguishes between merely hoping for progress and actively creating it. It's literally about paying yourself first. You review your calendar and prioritize your most important commitments to yourself by making daily deposits into your Blueprint account. These are firm, non-negotiable appointments with your future self, treated with the same importance as meetings with key clients. The most vital of these is your Blueprint Time a sacred period dedicated to deep, focused work that advances your vision. During this time, you establish the foundations. Just as an architect arranges key tasks to be carried out on the construction site, you plan your own key tasks through time blocking to turn your blueprint into reality.

- **Eliminate Distractions:** Your phone should be on silent and out of sight. Close unnecessary browser tabs. Turn off email notifications.

- **Focus on a Single Task:** Do not multitask. Dedicate the entire block to the "Primary Investment" you identified.

- **Honor the Appointment:** Treat this block like any other important commitment. If someone tries to schedule over it, respond with, "I'm sorry, I have another commitment at that time."

By scheduling these blocks, you are no longer hoping you will find time to work on your blueprint. You are intentionally *making* the time.

Step #3 - The Rule of Three & Protecting Your Fortress

Having a schedule filled with time blocks is a good start, but it can also feel overwhelming. A calendar packed from morning to night might seem more like a prison than a way to achieve freedom. That's where you need to introduce a system for focus and a strategy to protect your time. An architect's blueprint isn't just a list of every part of the building; it's a strategic plan that emphasizes the load-bearing walls, key pillars, and critical systems. The cosmetic details, while important, come later. Similarly, your schedule should revolve around your most essential projects. This is where a system for strategic focus and a fortress for tactical protection come into play. The "Rule of Three" is your system; learning to defend your time is your fortress. This combination ensures your schedule becomes a tool for liberation, not a cage you create for yourself. It allows you to dedicate your best energy to what matters most, while setting boundaries to work without constant interruptions. This is how to build a schedule that supports your vision, not the other way around..

- **The Rule of Three** - Your Weekly Focus System: You cannot do everything at once. The "Rule of Three" is a simple system to combat overwhelm. At the beginning of each week, you will define your three most important Blueprint priorities for the week ahead. These are the three things that, if you accomplish them, will make the week a definitive success. Then, each day, your "Primary Investment" should be a task that directly serves one of those three weekly priorities. This creates a clear hierarchy for your attention. It prevents you from getting lost in trivial tasks and ensures your most valuable Blueprint Time is always allocated to your most valuable work.

- **Protecting Your Time** - Defending Your Fortress: Your time-blocked schedule is your fortress, and the world will constantly try to breach its walls. You must become a vigilant defender. This does not mean being inflexible, but it does mean setting clear boundaries.

- **Learn to Say "No" Gracefully:** When a request conflicts with your Blueprint Time, a simple, "I'd be happy to help, but I'm in the middle of a deep-focus session. Can I get back to you this afternoon?" works wonders.

- **Batch Your "Maintenance" Tasks:** Group similar, low-focus tasks (like answering emails) into their own dedicated time blocks. This prevents them from constantly interrupting your high-focus Blueprint Time.

- **Communicate Your System:** Let colleagues and family know about your routine. "I'm dedicating 9-11 AM every morning to deep work, so I'll be offline, but I'll be fully available afterward." Managing expectations is key.

Winning the Day, Every Day

Leadership expert John Maxwell powerfully states, "Success is lost or found in your daily agenda." This is the core message of this chapter. The grand vision you hold for your life and the detailed blueprint you've designed all come down to the choices you make in the small, often overlooked moments of your daily routine. Success isn't something you randomly win like a lottery; instead, it's a structure you intentionally construct step by step.

Your daily schedule is like a construction site. Each day, you start with a new 24-hour block. You can choose to let the chaos of external events shape what gets built, leading to a disorganized collection of unfinished projects and lost resources. Alternatively, you can act as the architect, with a well-defined plan, deliberately constructing the elements that realize your vision. To do this successfully, you need to master two related skills: the ability to create **time** and the discipline to create **space**.

Creating **time** is not about magic. It is about the intentional, strategic allocation of your 24-hour deposit. The Architect Hour is your primary tool for this. It is the time you carve out for high-level thinking, reflection on the past and planning for the day ahead. This is not "doing time" but "thinking time." Amid the busy construction site with the noise of hammers and demanding crew, it's easy to lose sight of the big design picture. The architect needs moments to step back from the chaos, review the blueprints, and confirm that the work each day aligns with the overall vision. Your morning and evening routines serve this purpose; they are your dedicated times for clarity. Ignoring this is like a construction crew starting to build without guidance, with lots of activity, noise, and wasted resources, but with a messy final product. Allocating time for strategic review ensures your efforts are not just vigorous but also focused and effective.

Equally important is the discipline of creating space. Our lives are busy, filled with loved ones, family, friends, significant others, and various responsibilities. These are vital, lively parts of our lives' foundation. However, the architect cannot be on the construction site all the time. To stay focused and creative, you need to carve out space away from the noise. This space is the quiet environment, both physically and mentally, that you intentionally create. It can be a solo walk without your phone, a half-hour reading in a quiet room before anyone wakes, or a deliberate choice to decline social plans for a peaceful evening of recharging. Creating this space isn't selfish; it's a strategic act of self-care. In this quiet, you can hear your own voice, sort your thoughts, and reconnect with your "why." Without it, the constant noise around you will drown out your inner guidance, causing you to follow everyone else's expectations instead.

Time and space are the two pillars of your architectural studio. Time is for planning; space is for thinking. Together, they establish the focused, self-centered environment needed to stay on course. This is where you reaffirm your commitment to your blueprint, protected from distractions that could steer you off track. It's not about creating a strict, joyless schedule that locks you in a prison of productivity. Instead, it's about building a structure that frees you.

It's about developing a routine that automates important decisions, freeing up your mental and emotional energy to focus on the creative, challenging work of building. You've surveyed the land, designed your blueprint, and now you've rebuilt your routine to make room for construction. The life of an architect isn't built in a single moment of inspiration but in the accumulation of daily intentional focus.

Section Four

Build Phase: Build Your Way Forward

Chapter 10

From Dreamer to Builder

Let's take a moment to recognize the progress you've made. This is a significant achievement. You have delved into the challenging and often overlooked work of self-inquiry, a path many avoid their entire lives. You have grappled with questions of vision and purpose, exploring your inner self to discover a "why" that can serve as a steady anchor in any storm. You have also found your voice amid external noise and claimed your core right to be a creator, rather than just a consumer, of your life.

You have transitioned from internal exploration to external design. You have turned your vision into a practical plan, the first draft of your life's blueprint. This document is more than just a list of goals; it is a declaration of intent and a strategic map that links the coordinates of your current reality to the distant star of your future self. You have identified your models, those architects from afar whose presence inspires and guides you. You have taken a clear, honest look at the potential costs of building, understanding that anything of value must be paid for with the currencies of time, comfort, and ego. You have also reshaped your daily routine, transforming it from a chaotic reaction to the world's demands into an intentional system for creating the time and space needed for deep, meaningful work. You have completed the strategic work that transforms an idea of success into a tangible project, guided by tools, systems, and decisive actions to move you forward.

Your blueprint is no longer just a dream in your mind; it has become a tangible plan. It appears as a well-designed, inspiring stack of paper proof of your courage and clarity. It represents the promise you've made to yourself. However, at this moment, it remains merely a plan and a stack of paper, impressive but unproductive, as paper alone cannot build anything. No matter how sincere, a promise holds no weight until it's fulfilled through action. The final and most perilous illusion is believing that having a perfect plan equals making real progress. This illusion is a beautiful prison, where you can admire your life's blueprints without actually living them, feeling accomplished without taking any risks.

You've come too far; don't fall into the trap of lazy ambition. It's loving the idea of success but not wanting to do the messy, hard, and often humbling work required to bring your blueprint to life. Lazy ambition is wishing for the finished skyscraper but avoiding getting your hands dirty on the construction site. It's dreaming of the trophy but unwilling to show up for practice. It also involves sabotaging others' work to create shortcuts to advance your own. It is the desire for the outcome without committing to the process. If you let it, your blueprint right now could be the perfect example of lazy ambition. It's so easy to get attached to it. You can refine it, color-code it, share it with friends, and talk endlessly about the amazing vision of success you're about to create. This feels productive. It gives the illusion of progress and lets you maintain the identity of an ambitious architect while avoiding the fear of actually laying a brick. You gain the emotional reward of ambition without the real-world risk of trying to accomplish something you've never done before.

Don't be fooled. This is the most dangerous stage of your journey because it creates a false sense of achievement when you see the results of using our digital design studio to create your blueprint, tools, and systems. Your ideas have transitioned from your mind to visually appealing documents representing your desired future. Staring at a dynamic blueprint feels good, but it can lull you into a state of permanent inaction camouflaged by lazy ambition. Recognize this moment for what it is: the last gatekeeper between dreaming and building. Lazy ambition is that voice saying, "Let's review the plans again," and tempting you to do "just a little more research." It relies on the false idea that the perfect moment, perfect connection, or right sign will come before you start. It also shifts responsibility onto others and uses setbacks or setbacks as excuses to delay action. The architect knows that the only sign needed is the one on their desk, that says, "The construction site is open." Decisive, meaningful, and imperfect action is the only way to beat lazy ambition. Be willing to trade the deception of perfection for the messy, unpredictable, and challenging reality of doing the work.

Welcome to Part 4. This is the Build phase. Here, the ink of your blueprint meets the dirt of the real world. It's a change in state, like water turning to ice; the moment when the fluid world of ideas becomes the solid reality of action. This is where we move from planning your work to working your plan. The construction site of your life is now open. The materials have been delivered. The crew representing your mindsets, skills, and systems is on standby. But nothing happens until the architect gives the order to start. The journey from dreamer to architect isn't complete when you finish designing; it's complete when you lay the first brick.

Get Out of Your Head

If a great idea were all it took to transform our lives, we would all be living in a constant flow of wealth, fulfillment, and joy. But it takes much more than just a thought. It requires you to prioritize your preparation mindset every day. Defining your voice is empowering, and designing your blueprint is invigorating, but it all means nothing if you keep it locked inside your mind. You must build.

I don't know what it feels like to be physically imprisoned, but I know the feeling of being mentally trapped, locked in the cell of my own mind. When you convict yourself with self-doubt, overthinking, or procrastination, you imprison yourself. For many, success never comes not because it wasn't accessible, but because they don't take action. They let a lack of confidence and fear of other people's opinions prevent them from pursuing the life they want.

To discover your purpose, your ideas must shift from your mind into daily actions. Your destiny isn't something you choose; it's something you uncover. Still, you won't find the life you were meant to live if you're trapped in your own thoughts. Not every idea will succeed. You will face incredible wins, setbacks, and failures, but all of it is designed to give you the freedom, character, and direction you need.

Are you guilty of letting self-doubt and procrastination keep you trapped in your mind? You're not alone. These forces have held us all back at some point. The time is now to set yourself free. Success doesn't care about your excuses. The person you want to become can't be built on self-doubt; they must be built on the foundation of self-confidence, persistence, and continuous learning. The challenge isn't external; it's internal. You become an unstoppable force when you believe in yourself and refuse to give up your ability to create. The first obstacle is in our own minds. But you hold the key. You can either lock up your potential or unlock the possibilities of a life well-lived.

Set yourself free. Get out of your head. Turn your ideas into actions.

The Myth of the Perfect Plan

You have a blueprint in hand, and you can see the grand structure of success you want to build. But a powerful force keeps countless aspiring architects from ever breaking ground: the myth of the perfect plan. This myth is born from the conveyor-belt conditioning we have spent a lifetime internalizing. That system taught us that success comes from submitting a flawless final product, the perfect test, the perfect report, the perfect project. We were graded on the finished piece, not on the chaotic, iterative process of learning and discovery. This trains us to believe that any visible flaw is a sign of incompetence. As a result, we develop a deep-seated fear of being wrong, and the safest way to never be wrong is to never produce anything at all.

This myth whispers that your blueprint isn't quite ready yet. It urges you to do a bit more research, consider one more contingency, wait for perfect conditions, or seek one last wave of inspiration. It is a seductive lie because it masks fear as diligence. This trap is called analysis paralysis. It is the state of being so caught up in planning that you never actually start taking action. It leads to endless tweaking of the blueprint while the construction site remains empty. This is sophisticated self-sabotage. You maintain the identity of a hard-working architect committed to your project, all while safely avoiding the risk of failure in the real world. You are busy, but not building. You are engaged in planning rather than making progress. The perfect plan becomes a shield, protecting your ego from the inevitable bruises that come with real-world construction.

You must understand this: your blueprint isn't a sacred text to be perfected before you use it. It's a living document, your best hypothesis about the path forward based on the information you have today. It's a starting line, not a finish line. But the most valuable information you'll ever get won't come from more thinking; it comes from taking action and getting feedback. You'll learn more from laying the first ten bricks and seeing how they fit, how they feel, how they hold up than you will from ten more hours staring at the plans. The real world shows you the flaws and opportunities in your design that you could never see on paper. An architect who has never built anything is just a theorist. A true architect knows that the design is refined through the build. They welcome the unexpected challenges of the construction site because they understand that each problem solved makes them and their future designs better.

Pursue Progress, not Perfection

Just as you must abandon the myth of the perfect plan, you also need to let go of the idea of perfect action. Don't let perfection become the enemy of your progress. There's a misleading mindset that people with good intentions can fall into. It stems from lazy ambition: they proudly call themselves a "perfectionist." Let me be clear: this is a label you should refuse to adopt. Claiming to be a perfectionist is a socially acceptable mask for mindsets that keep you handcuffed by procrastination and overthinking, locked in the prison of your mind. It sounds like a strength "I just have very high standards", but it's actually a weakness. Often, it's a shield hiding a deep-rooted fear of failure, judgment, or the vulnerability of simply not being good enough yet.

As an architect, you are not chasing perfection; you are pursuing progress. Your daily goal is to move forward, one intentional action at a time. The pursuit of perfection is static; it waits for flawless conditions that will never come. The pursuit of progress is dynamic; it builds momentum. Think of it this way: perfection requires you to restart every time you don't succeed. Progress only asks that you get started. Progress urges you to fail forward, learning proactively from mistakes rather than being paralyzed by the excuses of perfection. Perfectionism disrupts the momentum that results from your commitment to decisive action because if you can't guarantee a perfect outcome, you hesitate to act at all.

Hesitation causes inconsistent growth because it makes you wait for perfect conditions before acting. You get motivated, take a few steps, hit a barrier, and then go back to the drawing board to "perfect" your approach, which kills your momentum. This unpredictable progress always comes from inconsistent action, which results from chasing an impossible standard. The pursuit of perfection stops you from experiencing the losses and lessons needed to successfully build your plan.

You must learn to embrace failure not as an indictment of your worth, but as an essential part of the building process. A master builder becomes a master not by never making a mistake, but by making thousands of mistakes and learning from every single one. Understanding that failure is possible, even probable, is the humility you must carry to stay aware that you are traveling to a place you've never been.

On your journey, you'll encounter both wins and losses. Regardless of the outcome, you must learn to extract lessons that make you stronger. Perfection isn't the goal. Failure is the tuition you pay for the insights and direction you need. You won't get everything right, and you shouldn't expect to. You're a continuous learner, and the goal is continuous growth over time. Progress is by no means an accidental; it's the hard-won result of pushing your limits, practicing patience to stay the course, and showing persistence even after setbacks.

Success is about playing the long game. Those who achieve it find ways to make small, steady progress every day.

Failure: An Ingredient for Success

During the building phase, every failure teaches a lesson that becomes part of your recipe for success. If you research your mentors and models, you'll notice a common theme in the lives of those who achieve their envisioned success: failure. It is a fundamental ingredient that some try to avoid, while others see it as an essential part of the journey.

A failure is not a final judgment; it's proof that you courageously attempted to create something from scratch. That's why, for the architect, failure is a more desirable goal than perfection.

Perfection is an illusion. It's the false belief that you are advancing when, in reality, you are just running in circles inside the prison of your mind, endlessly tweaking a plan you're too afraid to test. Failure, on the other hand, is concrete proof that you chose to act. It's the natural result of trying something new. It means you moved from overthinking to taking action in the real world. The action may not have yielded the outcome you hoped for, but it still produced a result. And that result is data. It's insight. It's a lesson you can use to improve your plan and your next move.

You must commit to never self-sabotaging your success by treating failure as an enemy. It is your most honest and valuable friend, the mentor who will tell you the truths others are too polite to say. And you will need this friend, because as you start to build, the voices of doubt will get louder. You will start to think:

- *"I see others moving so fast, and I question why I'm not there yet."* This is the trap of comparison. Remember, you are seeing their highlight reel, not their blooper reel. Your models are for inspiration, not for measurement. Your only job is to lay your next brick.

- *"I'm unsure if I have what it takes to get there."* This feeling is universal. No architect begins a massive project feeling 100% prepared. You don't need "what it takes" to build the skyscraper today. You only need what it takes to lay the first brick. Self-confidence isn't a prerequisite for starting; it's the result of starting..

- *"I frequently allow distractions to interrupt my focus."* This is not a character flaw; it is a sign that your systems need reinforcement. Every time you consciously choose your planned work over a distraction, you strengthen your muscle of focus.

- *"My inconsistent progress is my own doing."* This is a moment of powerful self-awareness, not self-condemnation.

Consistency is a skill, not a personality trait. Inconsistent progress is data telling you that the actions you've planned are likely too big. The antidote to inconsistency is to shrink the action.

- *"I feel like time is passing me by."* This is true. Time is passing for all of us. This feeling should not be a source of anxiety, but a source of urgency. The clock is ticking whether you are building or contemplating. Use this feeling not to rush your work, but to *start* it.

You should see these thoughts not as truths, but as the final defense mechanisms of your old self trying to keep you safe. Your role is to thank them for their concern and then, with decisive action, prove them wrong.

A failed action isn't a personal failure; it's a data point. Your task is to learn how to manage disappointment and extract the information that transforms your losses into lessons. After any setback, you should ask a new set of questions: "What did this experience teach me? What was the flaw in my strategy? What skill gap did this reveal? What will I do differently next time?" The person who can do this consistently is unstoppable.

Overcoming Disappointment

You've experienced it, and so has everyone else. Whether it's your favorite sports team losing the big game, being rejected by someone you're interested in, not getting your dream job or internship, or being denied admission to your preferred college, disappointment hurts. It also includes the pain when a loved one fails to keep a promise. Disappointment is a universal human emotion that emerges whenever our expectations are unmet. As an architect committed to taking decisive action, you *will* encounter disappointment. It is not a matter of if, but when.

How you handle disappointment reflects how you see yourself and your journey. Leadership expert Robin Sharma said, "Disappointment is the way life tests your commitment." It tests your dedication to yourself and your plan. During moments of opposition, most people tend to get stuck. You can't escape problems; they simply show up in different forms at every new stage. As an architect of your life, your goal isn't to find a path without obstacles but to have the confidence to face challenges as they come.

Think of it like a GPS in your car. If you encounter a detour, your goal is to reach your destination, not to get stuck because you missed the signs. Frustration and disappointment serve as signals from your internal GPS indicating that the current route is blocked. They aren't a judgment on your destination. The architect's role is to interpret these signals and adjust the plan without abandoning the original vision. Sometimes, obstacles can become stepping stones.

Disappointment can be an obstacle or an opportunity. The choice is yours. While disappointment is inevitable, choosing to be discouraged is optional. You don't have to sacrifice your joy and self-confidence for the discouragement and self-doubt that disappointment offers. Here are three principles to apply whenever you face the sting of a setback.

1. **Recognize and Release:** The first step is to acknowledge that you feel disappointed. You can't get past an emotion you're unwilling to face. Feel it. It's real. But recognition isn't the same as acceptance. It doesn't mean you have to let disappointment stay for a long time. Think of it as a knock at the door. You can acknowledge the knock without opening the door and letting the visitor in your space.

2. **Retrieve Feedback:** Once you have managed the initial emotional storm, the next step is to become a detective. Unpleasant as they are, disappointments are always filled with data. You must learn to see disappointment as an alarm that alerts you to opportunities for self-improvement. Highly successful people proactively seek feedback, while those who settle for mediocrity tend to fear it. Ask tough questions: What was the flaw in my strategy? What skill gap did this reveal? This process turns the sting of disappointment into a strategic review.

3. **Reset and Relaunch:** Finally, once you have identified the emotion and gathered the feedback, you must reset and relaunch. Disappointment is not meant to break you; it is meant to teach you. Resetting involves taking the feedback and intentionally directing your energy toward

a new strategy. With that new strategy in place, you must relaunch. Relaunching requires you to bravely re-engage in pursuing your goals, armed with new insight and a refined approach.

Decisive Action: Your Master Tool

In Chapter 7, you were introduced to the framework of Tools, Systems, and Actions. Your tools, like your schedule, are essential. Your systems, like the Architect Hour, are the scaffolding that supports your work. But Action is the primary tool. It is the hammer. It is the one tool that activates all the others. A schedule is useless if you don't act on it. A mentor's advice is worthless if you don't implement it. Action is the catalyst. Your plans hold possibilities, but only taking action can turn those possibilities into real results and sustainable progress.

This is why developing the skill of decisive action is essential. It doesn't mean acting recklessly. The conveyor-belt mindset often mixes up action with recklessness because it relies on waiting for permission. In contrast, the architect knows that decisive action involves giving yourself permission. It's about making the best decision possible with the available information and then taking steps forward, trusting your ability to adjust as needed. This approach is the best remedy for analysis paralysis, which traps dreamers in their own minds. Taking action is what opens the door to freedom.

Every time you take a small, decisive action, you do more than just complete a task. You cast a vote for the person you want to become. You build the most important part of your mindset: your self-confidence. Let's be clear: self-confidence isn't a feeling you wait for before you start; it's the feeling you create after you begin. It's something you act your way into. It's the result of seeing yourself make a decision and follow through. It's the internal record of your own reliability. Every action is a promise kept to yourself, and with each promise fulfilled, your trust in yourself grows. The dreamer waits to feel confident before acting, which means they never act. The architect acts despite lacking confidence, and in doing so, they build the very confidence they need to keep going.

How to Lay Your First Brick

So, how do you get started? You don't begin by trying to build the entire foundation all at once. Instead, you start by laying a single, manageable brick. This is the moment to turn all your planning into action. To defeat the overwhelming feeling of looking at your entire blueprint, you need to zoom in so closely that you're only focusing on one brick. This is your Smallest Viable Action (SVA). It's the absolute smallest, least intimidating physical step you can take today to move one of your priorities forward. The key is to make it so small that the excuses and fears in your mind have nothing to cling to.

Take out your blueprint. Look at your "Rule of Three" weekly priorities. Pick one. Now, ask yourself: *"What is the two-minute version of this task? What is the first physical step?"*

- If your priority is "Develop my communication skills," the SVA is not "Become a great public speaker." It is "Spend two minutes researching one local Toastmasters club."

- If your priority is "Find a mentor," the SVA is not secure a mentorship. It is spend two minutes drafting one sentence that describes what I would ask a mentor for.

- If your priority is "Start a side hustle," the SVA is not "Launch an online store." It is spend two minutes writing down five potential names for my business.

Do you see the power in this? The Smallest Viable Action isn't about making massive progress. It's about breaking inertia. Its main purpose is to get you off the starting block.

Graduating from SVAs to Daily Bricks

The SVA serves as your secret weapon against procrastination, but it's not the actual work. An architect doesn't construct a skyscraper with countless quick actions. Instead, they build it by placing heavy bricks repeatedly over time. Your aim is to transition from the SVA to focusing on laying Daily Bricks. A Daily Brick is a meaningful, concentrated work segment that shows real progress on your project. This is where your systems come into play.

Your Architect Hour is dedicated to identifying the Daily Brick you should focus on. Based on your weekly "Rule of Three" priorities, you determine your "Primary Investment" for the day, which is your Daily Brick. Your Time Block Schedule is the method you use to set aside dedicated, protected time on your calendar to work on that brick. This is your scheduled "Blueprint Time."

Let's revisit our examples:

- "Develop my communication skills": The SVA was finding a Toastmasters club. The Daily Brick is the one-hour time block you schedule to attend the Toastmasters club meeting.

- "Find a mentor": The SVA was drafting one sentence. The **Daily Brick** is the 45-minute time block you schedule to research five potential mentors and send each a personalized request.

- "Start a side hustle": The SVA was writing down names. The **Daily Brick** is the 90-minute time block you schedule to do a competitive analysis on your top name.

The SVA is what you use on days you feel resistance. It's the small step that gets you started. But the goal is to consistently show up for your scheduled time blocks and lay the Daily Bricks that create the real momentum needed to bring your blueprint to life. The journey from dreamer to architect isn't a single leap. It's a bridge you build, one Daily Brick at a time. The vision you have for your life is worth building. Your blueprint is solid. Now, there's only one thing left to do.

Close this book. Look at your plan. Identify your Smallest Viable Action.

Chapter 11

The Architect's Diet

You have laid your first brick. You have made the courageous leap from the world of ideas into the world of action. This is a moment worth celebrating, but it is also a time of great responsibility. The shift from designer to builder is a key transition in any architect's journey. On the construction site, intentions don't matter; only execution counts.

As you stand here, ready to work, you must face a fundamental truth that will determine the success of your entire project: the quality of your build depends on the quality of your materials. An architect who uses cheap, flimsy, or poorly sourced materials isn't just creating an inferior structure; they are setting up a future failure.

No matter how brilliant the blueprint, a skyscraper built with brittle steel and crumbling concrete is destined to collapse. Conversely, an architect who studies masterpieces and, more importantly, understands the high-grade materials that made them possible will bring a higher standard and a richer toolkit to their own designs. They know that what you build with is just as important as what you build.

This chapter emphasizes becoming your own supplier and quality control manager. Instead of using steel and concrete, the building blocks of your life are the ideas, information, and inspirations you process daily. Imagine your mind as a sophisticated algorithm an advanced, self-learning neural network continually trained by the data you provide. Every article, video, podcast, and conversation acts as a data point that shapes its programming. The information you intake today directly influences the thoughts, connections, and opportunities it will generate tomorrow. This is a real neurological process, not just metaphorical. The rule of "garbage in, garbage out" applies here: if you feed your mind low-quality, distracting, or negative data, it will produce similar thoughts, leading to anxiety, comparison, and procrastination. It will create a life you don't want, simply because that's the only blueprint it has received.

The essential question now is whether you're intentionally training your algorithm with high-quality, blueprint-aligned data, or simply letting the world supply it with digital junk. This issue is more pressing than ever because you're not in a neutral environment. The digital space isn't a well-organized library for your learning; it's a battlefield for your attention. Major forces vying for your focus aren't interested in your growth; they're focused on distracting you. Each social media feed, streaming service, and news alert represents a competing algorithm, designed with billion-dollar precision to hijack your mental patterns for profit. Their aim is to keep you scrolling, watching, and clicking, conditioning your mind to crave the next hit of dopamine, the next jolt of outrage, the next piece of trivial information. They are actively trying to feed your algorithm junk data because it's profitable. As the architect, you cannot remain a passive participant in this battle. You must become a conscious, strategic, and ruthless curator of your data inputs. This should be your top priority each day. While focusing on your daily priorities and the actions needed to accomplish them, make sure you are gathering information that provides the data you need to succeed as the architect of your life.

The Consumption Trap: Entertainment as an Anesthetic

We live in the Information Age, which is both a blessing and a curse. Never before in history has humanity had such unrestricted access to the collective knowledge of the human race. The answer to almost any question or a guide to any skill is just a click away. This is the blessing. The curse, however, is a digital system designed not for your education, but for your distraction. Our capitalist society, driven by profit, has leveraged technology to construct a system that makes it seductively easy to distract yourself from a stressful day, an unfulfilling job, and life's overall challenges.

This is the Consumption Trap. It's the endless, carefully curated loop of social media updates, viral videos, and celebrity gossip meant to keep us in a constant state of distraction. We pick up our phones for a single purpose, only to find ourselves an hour later, emerging from a digital fog and unsure of what we originally sought. It's important to recognize what's really occurring during these moments: you aren't just "relaxing." You're using entertainment as a form of anesthesia.

In a hospital, anesthesia is a carefully regulated drug used to temporarily eliminate sensation by blocking pain signals, allowing surgery to take place. You willingly undergo short periods of unconsciousness for a benefit. In contrast, digital anesthesia operates differently: no doctor controls the dosage, and nothing is healing during the process. Instead of providing temporary numbness for a lasting benefit, digital anesthesia involves accepting a constant, mild numbness to avoid everyday discomfort, stress, and decisions that push you outside your comfort zone. Unfortunately, most people find comfort by hiding in their social media feeds instead of doing the work to find the next version of themselves they need to become to achieve a fulfilling life they feel proud and excited about.

This digital anesthetic doesn't just block the immediate pain of a tough day; it also cuts off the nerves that carry the ache of unmet potential to your mind and heart. It's a deliberate attack on the discomfort that drives us to grow. Remember the sting from the "knowing-doing gap" in Chapter 6? That space between who you are and who you wish to be is meant to hurt a little. That pain acts as a catalyst, producing dissatisfaction and signaling your future self that it's time to get to work. Entertainment as an anesthetic dulls this signal, turning the sharp, motivating sting into a dull, tolerable throb that you can live with indefinitely. It lets you recognize the gap without feeling the need to close it right away. This is how years pass by, your vision of the blueprint fades, and you stop living as the architect of your own life. The anesthetic suppresses the inner voice you discovered in Chapter 5, the one that whispers, "You were made for more than this." Your true voice is a subtle signal, only audible when you dedicate the time and space to listen to it. The digital world is filled with constant noise and an endless flow of others' voices, opinions, and content, all designed to be as loud as possible. By immersing yourself in this nonstop stream, your internal voice gets drowned out, and you lose touch with your unique frequency. The anesthetic causes you to forget what your ambition sounds and looks like.

Most dangerously, it blurs your vision. It makes it harder to see the stark reality of your **"You Are Here" dot**, the critical starting coordinate you established with your internal GPS. An endless scroll through curated highlight reels distorts your perception of your own reality, making your messy, beautiful, and authentic starting point feel inadequate. It replaces the clear data of your self-assessment with the fuzzy, distorted data of comparison. This makes it difficult to plan effectively. An architect must be fully engaged and aware. You need to feel the texture of your challenges, identify the cracks in your foundation, and listen to the feedback from the world around you. These are not obstacles to avoid; they are essential data for your build. An anesthetized architect is absent and disconnected, a designer who refuses to visit their own site. You can't create your masterpiece if you're unconsciously stuck in feeds, watching others bring their plans to life.

The true cost isn't just the time lost, though that can be substantial. Every hour spent on mindless consumption is an hour you could have invested in your blueprint. It's a zero-return activity; once the time is gone, you can't get it back. Your time, a vital asset, has been wasted. Even more valuable is your attention needed to build momentum, clarity, and energy crucial for architects working on their blueprints. This includes the book you didn't read, the skill you didn't develop, and the connections you missed. The conveyor-belt world favors consumers. A passive, distracted audience is easier to manage and market to. But you are not a consumer; you are a creator. As an architect, you cannot ignore the reality of your construction site.

The Creator's Mandate: To Consume or to Create?

Shakespeare's timeless question was "To be, or not to be?" For the modern architect, the question must be transformed: "To consume, or to create?" This is not just a philosophical debate; it's a core operational choice that will shape who you are and influence your future. Every small decision you make about where to focus your attention answers this question repeatedly each day. This choice influences your attitude toward the world. A consumer acts as a passive observer, standing on the sidelines of their own life. Their default mode is to 'receive'; they wait to be entertained, informed, or directed. The creator, on the other hand, is an active participant, an agent in the field. Their default state is generate. Their posture is one of initiating a new project, starting a new conversation, or developing a new idea. This choice, made in the micro-moments of your day, determines whether you are ultimately a product of your environment or the architect of it. The five minutes waiting for your coffee: do you consume a feed of curated outrage, or do you create a note in your phone about a new idea for your project? The 30-minute commute: do you listen to celebrity gossip on the radio, or do you consume an audiobook that enhances a skill on your development plan? The evening on the couch: do you watch three hours of a series, or do you draft the first version of that proposal you've been putting off? Each choice is a small vote cast for the identity you are building. These votes, combined over time, determine who you ultimately become.

This is the Creator's Mandate, which rests on a simple, unchangeable rule: what you consume influences what you create. Just like a chef needs top-tier ingredients to make a world-class dish, an architect's mind is shaped by the quality of the information, ideas, and inspiration it receives. Relying only on fast food-like content limits your palate and hampers your ability to innovate, leading to creations that reflect the poor input. To build a life of purpose and fulfillment, feed your mind with high-quality knowledge. Your output will mirror your consumption dieting on digital junk results in subpar work, while a diet of excellence breeds excellence. This mandate emphasizes a clear boundary between two forms of consumption: **Education and Entertainment.**

Entertainment is consumption designed to distract you from your current reality. It is passive. It asks nothing of you but to watch, scroll, or listen. Its main goal is to help you pass the time and experience temporary sensations like amusement, outrage, or excitement. It is the mental equivalent of junk food. A little moderation can be a pleasant distraction, but a diet primarily made up of entertainment will leave your mind malnourished, sluggish, and unable to handle the hard work needed to build a meaningful life.

This passivity is the most dangerous part of the trap. It does more than just waste your time; it trains your mind to do nothing. Every hour spent binge-watching a series is an hour spent practicing the skill of being a spectator. You are conditioning your brain to receive, not create. You are strengthening neural pathways for observation and weakening those for creation. Over time, this creates a deep resistance to the kind of effort an architect or anyone aiming to build something meaningful must do. The heavy lifting of creating your life focused effort, wrestling with complex problems, and taking risks to create something new, starts to feel not just hard but unnatural. Your mind, used to the quick dopamine hits from passive entertainment, pushes back against any task that requires sustained, focused effort. This is why choosing to prioritize partying over studying can be so costly for college students. It's not just about getting a lower grade; it's about reinforcing an identity as a consumer of experiences rather than a creator of value.

For young professionals, nightly watching of a streaming series isn't just relaxation; it's nightly training in passivity, making it harder to show up the next day with the proactive energy needed to break free from an unfulfilling entry-level job. These aren't just zero-return investments; they are negative-return investments.

You're not just failing to build your future; you're actively diminishing your present.

Education, on the other hand, is a form of consumption meant to help you invest in your future. It is active; it requires your engagement and critical thinking. Its primary purpose isn't to pass the time and expand your capacity. It's the mental equivalent of nutrient-rich whole foods, fueling sustained energy, growth, and strength.

This active process of engagement is a form of mental construction. When you read a challenging book, you're not simply absorbing words; you're building new neural pathways, developing new frameworks for thinking, and assembling tools for your intellectual toolkit. Listening to a podcast by a leader in your field isn't just passive; it's an apprenticeship, reverse-engineering their mindset and strategies. This is how you actively train your mental algorithm. You feed it complex, high-resolution data needed for sophisticated outputs. You teach it to recognize patterns of success, spot opportunities others overlook, and solve problems with creativity that a mind fed on junk food could never match. Every moment spent on educational consumption is a direct investment in your blueprint, an investment that compounds over time like money.

For college students, this means consciously skipping one party each month to attend a guest lecture by an industry leader, not for extra credit, but for insight. It's choosing to use office hours to clarify exam points and build relationships with professors who are masters of their craft. For young professionals, it means realizing that while formal education may be over, your real education has just begun. Investing in a ticket to a professional conference rather than a concert shows an understanding that the connections and knowledge gained will be valuable long after the music has faded.

I am not suggesting you do not make time to engage in entertainment activities making a conscious shift from a diet of entertainment to a diet of education is an important part of your success during the building phase. This is the core of continuous learning. To make this process actionable, transition from being a passive consumer to an active curator.

Your **Skill Development Plan** is a tool that serves this purpose think of it as your architect's nutritional plan. It represents a deliberate strategy to source high-quality information needed to strengthen your mental and practical skills. This simple document outlines 3 to 5 key skill areas crucial for closing the "knowing-doing gap." You also select learning sources such as books, podcasts, courses, or models and allocate time to engage with them.

Your Skill Development Plan tells you *what* to build yourself with, and your daily routine ensures you have the *time* to do the building. This plan integrates directly with the daily routine you built in the last chapter. You can list your curriculum on paper, or you can use the Skill Builder tool at ***FindingTheNextYou.com/skills*** to actively track your progress. Use the Architect's Canvas to pin the articles and videos you discover, transforming your consumption into a curated library.

The Architect's Library:
A Practical Guide to Conscious Consumption

To understand the profound importance of building your own mental library, we should consider the story of Andrew Carnegie. As a young boy, born into poverty in Scotland and immigrating to the United States, his future of working grueling 12-hour days in a Pittsburgh cotton mill seemed inevitable. He was a cog in the machine of the Industrial Revolution, a world where access to knowledge was a luxury strictly reserved for the wealthy. Books were expensive, private possessions, locked away in the homes of the elite. For a poor boy like Andrew, the idea of a library was as distant as the moon. But a single, extraordinary act of generosity changed his life's course. A local man of means, Colonel James Anderson, did something revolutionary for the time: he opened his personal library of 400 books to the young boy, free of charge. For young Andrew, this was not just a room full of books; it was a door swung wide open to another universe previously blocked by the circumstances of his economic status.

In those volumes, borrowed carefully each week, Carnegie absorbed the ideas of the greatest minds in history literature, science, philosophy, economics. He wasn't just reading; he was shaping a new version of himself, brick by intellectual brick. He understood that information, knowledge, and organized thought were the keys that could unlock the prison of his circumstances. This dedication to relentless self-education became the foundation upon which he built one of the largest industrial empires the world has ever seen.

Rising from bobbin boy to telegraph operator, and eventually to the undisputed leader of the American steel industry, Carnegie became a true titan of his era. At his peak, his net worth was estimated to be the equivalent of over $300 billion today, making him one of the wealthiest people in history. His journey proved the power of knowledge combined with relentless action.

However, the most impactful part of Carnegie's story isn't what he made in steel; it is in books. Remembering the deep impact of Colonel Anderson's small library, a rare act of kindness in an era when education was a privilege for the wealthy and aware that his own experience was unusual, Carnegie set out on one of the greatest charity efforts in history: to create a system of over 2,500 free public libraries nationwide and worldwide. Carnegie is the visionary behind starting the movement of building libraries across our country.

He fundamentally believed that access to information was not a privilege, but a right, the essential fuel for any individual seeking to build a better life, regardless of their background. He solved the problem of access for generations to come, democratizing knowledge in an unprecedented way.

Today, you have a device in your pocket that offers instant access to more information than all the libraries Carnegie ever created, combined. The library is always open, with doors unlocked, and knowledge is free and plentiful. We are living in an era of unprecedented access, the very future Carnegie envisioned. However, ironically, we now face a different kind of poverty, perhaps even more dangerous than the one Carnegie escaped: a poverty of attention.

This is truly a fascinating paradox of our times. We've managed to overcome the challenge of access, yet in doing so, we've inadvertently introduced the issue of distraction. We have a world of education at our fingertips, yet we overwhelmingly opt for entertainment. As the architect of your life, you must be brutally honest about this choice. What does the latest celebrity gossip help you build? How does mastering the latest TikTok dance contribute to the foundation of the life you want to create? The answer, if you are honest, is that they build nothing.

The following steps are not just about cleaning up your social media feeds. They are about honoring the legacy of those who fought to give you the access you now take for granted.

1. Conduct an Information **Consumption Diet Audit.** For the next three days, be a neutral observer of your own consumption habits. Use a simple notebook. Every time you consume a piece of content, write it down and categorize it as either "E" for Education (it directly relates to your blueprint goals) or "T" for Entertainment. At the end of the three days, be honest with yourself. What is the ratio? This is your "before" picture. If you prefer, you can also utilize the design studio to access a digital version of the tool at: ***FindingTheNextYou.com/diet***

2. Curate Your Feeds. Go through every account you follow. For each one, ask: "Does this account consistently leave me feeling inspired and educated, or drained and distracted?" If it is the latter, be ruthless. Unfollow. Mute. Unsubscribe. This is not an act of judgment; it is an act of protection. Immediately after, intentionally follow the models you identified in Chapter 8 the industry leaders, the thinkers, the builders.

3. Build Your Personal Curriculum.

- **Build Your Reading List:** Based on your skill gaps, identify the top three books that can help you close them. Schedule the time to read them.

- **Curate Your Podcast Library:** Find the top podcasts in your field. Subscribe to them and delete the ones that are purely entertainment. Your commute can be transformed into a mobile classroom.

- **Invest in a Course:** Identify one high-quality online course that can accelerate your learning in a key area. Committing a small financial investment often dramatically increases your commitment.

By taking these steps, you are no longer a passive victim of the algorithm. You are the head librarian of your own mind.

How Consumption Fuels Creation

As you start to intentionally curate your information diet, a significant shift will begin to unfold. You will transition from a passive to an active state. This is the virtuous cycle of the architect, the driving force behind your lifelong growth and contribution. This isn't just a side-effect of your work; it is the ultimate reward.

The journey begins with a revolutionary move from being a mindless Consumer to an intentional Curator. This is an act of rebellion. You are deliberately rejecting the algorithm's effort to define your interests and instead applying your own blueprint. You stop being a passive victim of the feed and start controlling your own information flow. You are no longer just scrolling; you are strategically collecting intelligence, sourcing the specific, high-quality materials your design needs.

This act of curation naturally and inevitably leads to the next stage: you become a Creator. Creation is the ultimate act of learning, the final and most important step in the process. You can read ten books on a subject, but you'll never understand it as deeply as when you are forced to synthesize, apply, or teach it to someone else. As you consume higher-quality information, your mind, now a well-trained algorithm, will start to generate outputs. It will overflow with new connections, ideas, and solutions. The urge to do something with these ideas will become irresistible. This is where you must begin creating, even on a small, imperfect scale..

- Did you just finish a powerful book? Don't just put it on the shelf. **Create** a one-page summary of the key ideas and, most importantly, list three actions you will take this week to apply them.

- Did you listen to an inspiring interview with one of your models? Don't just think, "That was interesting." **Create** a LinkedIn post sharing your biggest takeaway and how it challenges a common assumption in your field.

- Are you learning a new skill from an online course? Don't just watch the videos and take the quiz. **Create** a small, personal project where you are forced to apply what you have learned to solve a real problem.

These small acts of creation aren't meant for an audience; they're for you. They serve as the process of digesting the information you take in, transforming the abstract fuel of knowledge into the concrete strength of understanding. This is the essential step to genuinely owning what you learn. Without it, you're merely a collector of interesting facts, like a librarian with a lovely but unused collection. When you engage in this process, you become a builder.

This brings us to the final, inspiring stage: the upward spiral. This cycle drives "Finding The Next You." The more high-quality information you take in, the more motivated and prepared you are to create. Creating more leads to learning more, developing new skills, and building genuine self-confidence, not just shallow affirmations, but resilient confidence earned through demonstrated competence. As your confidence and skills increase, your vision becomes more ambitious and refined. A bigger, more ambitious vision encourages you to seek even higher-quality, more challenging information. This creates a virtuous cycle where consumption fuels creation. As an architect of your life, be intentional with what you consume, because it directly inspires your ability to create.

Chapter 12

The Architect's Field Guide

Think of this chapter as your emergency kit. The journey of building a life is long, and the inspiration you feel right now will inevitably fade. There will be days when the fog rolls in, and you lose sight of your North Star, or when the noise of the conveyor belt threatens to drown out your own voice. When that happens, you don't need to re-read the entire book; you need to return here. This is your personal operating system, distilled into its most potent form. It is the reference manual designed to help you recalibrate, reset, and relaunch whenever you drift off course.

At the beginning of this book, we established a fundamental truth: the world is full of opportunities for those with the mindset to define and pursue their own vision for success. For most of your life, you may have unconsciously followed society's rules, living inside a box that confines you to the rules of an obsolete economy.

The educational system gives you a syllabus, the corporate world gives you a ladder; both provide the comforting illusion of a clear path. But you have awakened to the reality that this path, while seemingly safe, often leads to a quiet, unfulfilling destination of disappointment. You have recognized the invisible walls of the box and have chosen to find the door.

The purpose of this chapter is to distill everything you have learned into a single, powerful, and repeatable strategy. Consider this your **Architect's Field Guide**.

This is the one chapter you can, and should, return to again and again. It is your playbook, a reference manual for the lifelong practice of intentional life design. When you feel yourself drifting, stuck in a cycle of procrastination, when the noise of the world drowns out your own voice, or when you lose sight of your North Star in the fog of life's challenges, you will return to this chapter. It is here that you will recalibrate your strategy and refocus your efforts on what truly matters.

Up to this point, our focus has been on understanding and designing. But the goal was never to give you interesting ideas to think about; it was to fundamentally change how you operate in the world. We are now making the final, most important shift: from understanding to daily practice.

The ultimate measure of your success as an architect will not be how well you can talk about these concepts, but how consistently you can live them. True transformation does not happen in a moment of inspiration; it happens in the succession of a thousand ordinary days lived with extraordinary intention.

The DEFINE Strategy - Anchoring Your "Why"

The Core Principle: Your Vision is Your North Star

The entire practice of being a life architect begins with one foundational act: defining your vision. For centuries, sailors navigating treacherous seas relied on one constant: Polaris, the North Star. Storms could rage, and waves could crash, but as long as they could find that one fixed point of light, they were never truly lost. Your vision serves this exact purpose. It is the unchanging point of light in your personal sky that guides your every decision. It is the ultimate source of your motivation, the deep, resonant "why" that will pull you through the inevitable challenges of any meaningful construction project.

This is the essence of Finding The Next You. To close the gap between where you are today and where you desire to be, an evolution must occur. You cannot arrive at a new destination as the same person who started the journey. The person you are today has precisely the life that your current skills, mindset, and habits have built. To build something different, you must become different. You must become the *Next You*. Who is this "Next You"? This is the you that is no longer paralyzed by the fear of other people's opinions. This is the you that is fiercely committed to investing your time wisely, choosing education over distraction. This evolution is not a matter of chance; it is a matter of design. And that design starts with the crystal-clear definition of your North Star.

Key Concepts Revisited: To define an authentic vision, you must anchor it in two concepts. First, **You Were Created to Create.** Your journey is not a scavenger hunt for a pre-written destiny someone else has hidden for you. You are an active creator, not a passive recipient. Defining your vision is your ultimate creative project, the moment you transition from being a character in someone else's story to the author of your own. The entire conveyor-belt system is designed to turn you into a consumer, a consumer of knowledge, a consumer of instructions, a consumer of a pre-packaged life. This first principle is your declaration of independence from that system. It is the recognition that your most fundamental human drive is not to consume, but to create. This isn't about artistic talent; it is about the act of bringing something new into existence that did not exist before: a new solution, a new system, a new path. Your vision is the first and most important of these creations. It is the act of looking at the blank canvas of your future and having the courage to make the first stroke.

Second, **Finding Your Voice.** An effective North Star cannot be a borrowed light; it must be a star that burns from within. Your vision must be authentically yours, built from your own values and desires, not the "shoulds" and "supposed-tos" of the world. This is often the most difficult work because those external voices from parents, society, and social media are not just outside of you; they are inside of you. They have become the critical inner narrator that questions your ambition and judges your dreams. Finding your voice is an act of excavation. It is the process of digging through the layers of other people's expectations to unearth the core of what *you* truly want. A borrowed vision has no power. It is a weak, flickering light that the first storm of doubt or criticism will extinguish. An authentic vision, however, born from your own voice, resonates with a unique frequency. It has its own gravitational pull, a force that will keep you oriented and moving forward, even when the path is dark, and you are navigating by faith alone.

The Essential Tool: Your Guiding Questions

Your primary tool for the DEFINE strategy is the set of Guiding Questions from Chapter 8. These are not questions to be answered once and filed away; to do so is to revert to the conveyor-belt mindset of completing a one-time assignment. Instead, you must see them for what they are: a lifelong strategic tool for maintaining clarity. Think of these questions as the architect's surveying instruments. A surveyor does not just map the land once at the beginning of a project. They return to their instruments repeatedly throughout the build to check alignments, confirm elevations, and ensure the structure being built precisely matches the blueprint's intent. Your Guiding Questions serve this exact function for your life. They are your diagnostic tool for preventing "architectural drift," the slow, almost imperceptible deviation from your original vision that can happen amidst the daily chaos of construction. By revisiting these questions, you are placing your transit on the foundation of your "why" and taking a fresh reading of your current position. This is how you ensure that the life you are busy building is still the life you set out to create. The core questions explore the key domains of a well-built life:

- Who do you want to be in your career?

- What type of person do you want to become?

- How do you want to show up in your relationships?

- Who do you want to impact?

- What type of legacy do you want to build?

- How much money do you want to make?

Call to Action: Your Quarterly Board Meeting

As the architect of your life, you must regularly review your master plan to ensure the structure you are building is still the one you want to live in. Therefore, you must schedule a recurring "strategic review" with yourself once every quarter. Put it on your calendar as a non-negotiable appointment. Think of any successful enterprise; it operates with a rhythm of strategic review. A board of directors meets quarterly to hold the CEO accountable, analyze performance against projections, and make high-stakes decisions about the company's future. Your life is the most important enterprise you will ever run. To treat it with less seriousness and to operate without a formal process of review and accountability is architectural malpractice. When you stepped off the conveyor belt, you gave up the built-in, external review systems of grades and annual performance reviews. You are now the CEO, Chairman, and sole board member of your life's enterprise; this quarterly meeting is the most important one on your calendar. To skip it is an act of gross negligence against your most important stakeholder: your future self. This is your formal process for high-level course correction, preventing the slow, almost imperceptible drift that can pull you miles off course over time if left unchecked.

1. **Review:** Read your original answers to the Guiding Questions out loud. Reconnect with the ambition you felt.

2. **Reflect:** Look back over the past 90 days. How have your actions aligned with these answers? Where did you drift? Be honest, not judgmental.

3. **Reframe:** Ask: "Are these answers still true for me?" Your core values may be constant, but the expression of your vision may evolve. Reaffirm what is still true; have the courage to refine what is not.

4. Re**solve:** Based on your reflection, set one to three key objectives for the next 90 days.

Daily Integration: The "Future Self" Anchor

A quarterly review provides high-level strategic alignment. But a strategy is useless if it isn't present in your daily decisions. Your "Future Self" letter is the tool for daily integration. It is your compass on the deck, the small, powerful instrument you consult to make the thousand tiny course corrections that keep a ship on its long journey. Understand that the first moments of your day are a battleground for your attention. From the second you wake, the world is desperate to set your agenda. Your email inbox, your social media feed, the breaking news they are all armies attempting to storm the shores of your focus, pulling you into a state of reaction before you have even had a chance to act. They want you to spend your day putting out their fires and responding to their priorities. The daily integration of your vision is a proactive, defiant act. It is you planting your flag on the shores of your own morning and declaring, with absolute authority, that you will set the agenda for your day. This is the first, and most important, victory. It is the choice to be the cause of your day, not the effect of it.

Actionable Habit: The Two-Minute Anchor

In corporate a two-minute review of your "Future Self" letter into your morning Architect Hour.

- **Minute 1: Read and Feel.** Read your letter or vision statement. Don't just skim the words; inhabit the feeling behind them.

- **Minute 2: Connect and Commit.** Ask yourself: "What is one choice I can make today that the person in this letter would be proud of?"

The DESIGN Strategy - Building Your Blueprint

The Core Principle: Your Blueprint is Your Living Roadmap

If the DEFINE strategy is about finding your North Star, the DESIGN strategy is about drawing the map that will guide you. Your blueprint is your living roadmap, the strategic plan that connects your current reality, your "You Are Here" dot, to your future vision. A vision without a blueprint is a destination without a map; it's a beautiful idea that is likely to remain forever out of reach because it has no connection to the ground.

It is crucial to understand the two most important words in this principle: *living* and *roadmap*. It is a **roadmap**, not a rigid set of turn-by-turn directions. The conveyor belt gives you turn-by-turn directions; it tells you exactly where to go and how to get there because the path is already paved. The architect, however, works in the unpaved wilderness. A roadmap for an explorer does not show every twist and turn; it marks the key landmarks, the mountain ranges to cross, the rivers to ford, and the general direction of travel. It provides structure and clarity, but it trusts the explorer's ability to navigate the specific terrain they encounter. Your blueprint serves this purpose. It empowers you with clear direction while honoring your intelligence and adaptability to handle unexpected obstacles that a pre-written set of directions could never anticipate.

Furthermore, your blueprint is **living**, not static. A static plan assumes you have perfect knowledge at the beginning of your journey. An architect knows this is a fool's errand. A real architectural blueprint is often revised during construction. When builders hit an unexpected pipe or discover unforeseen structural issues, they don't abandon the project; they go back to the blueprint, make the necessary adjustments, and continue the build. Your life's blueprint must be treated with the same dynamic respect. It is a working document, a first draft designed to be refined by the feedback you get from the real world. Every action you take is a test of your initial hypothesis. A revision is not a sign of a flawed design; it is a sign of an intelligent architect who is actively learning from the construction process. This is what separates the architect from the rigid follower of rules. The follower panics when reality doesn't match the plan. The architect adapts the plan to master reality.

Key Concepts Revisited: To design an effective roadmap, you must constantly engage with two critical concepts that serve as the twin engines of your design process. Think of them as the operating system and the power source for your architectural software. First, **The Internal GPS.** This is your operating system. Your blueprint is the physical manifestation of this guidance system. Your values are the fixed satellites that establish your non-negotiable boundaries, and your preparation mindset is the algorithm that calculates your path within those boundaries. Your GPS ensures your design has integrity. Second, **The Architect's Diet (Consume to Create).** This is your power source. The quality of your design will be a direct reflection of the quality of the information you consume. A mind fed on a diet of distraction and junk data will produce a flimsy, uninspired design. A mind fed on a diet of intentional learning and high-quality ideas will produce a sophisticated and resilient one. Your design process is fed by your consumption process. One provides the structure, the other provides the substance.

The Essential Tools & Activities:

- **The Personal GPS Calibration:** This is the architect's mandatory "site survey." Your honest assessment of your Skills, Mindset, Environment, and Resources provides the unvarnished truth of your "You Are Here" dot.

- **The Architect's Blueprint Design Session:** This is the core drafting process where you identify your Strategic Pillars, conduct your Gap Analysis, and identify your Key Materials (skills and knowledge).

- **The Skill Development Plan:** This is your "materials list" for the construction project, your proactive plan for acquiring the knowledge and competencies your design requires.

Daily Integration: The "Evening Review" Refinement

Just as the DEFINE strategy is integrated into your morning, the DESIGN strategy is built into your evening. If the morning is about setting your direction, the evening is about reviewing your course and refining your map for tomorrow. This is arguably one of the most critical habits in your entire operating system, as it's where learning and adaptation happen. Without this daily review, the day's events, both good and bad, simply fade into the background noise. Small wins are forgotten and fail to build confidence. Small mistakes or setbacks are ignored, only to be repeated, leading to frustration and the false conclusion that "this isn't working." The evening review is the disciplined act of capturing this data before it disappears, transforming every day into a lesson. It is the process that allows you to fail forward intelligently, rather than just failing. The conveyor-belt mindset encourages you to simply forget a hard day and "start fresh" tomorrow. The architect knows that a day, no matter how difficult, is a priceless source of feedback. To "start fresh" without first extracting the lessons is to willingly repeat your mistakes. By becoming a detective of your own daily performance, you uncover the subtle patterns, the hidden obstacles, and the surprising strengths that are invisible in the rush of the moment. This habit turns every day into a strategic feedback loop, ensuring that you end each day slightly wiser than when you began.

Actionable Habit: Review daily the 4-Point Inspection "Reflect, Reset, Refocus, and Relaunch"

Position the "Reflect, Reset, Refocus, and Relaunch" portion of your evening Architect Hour as your Daily Blueprint Review. Each day, your actions produce results. These results are invaluable, real-world data. Your evening routine is when you bring that data back to the design studio.

- **Reflect (Analyze the Data):** Compare the day's "as-built" reality to your original plans. What was the outcome of your actions? Did you encounter an unexpected obstacle?

- **Reset (Accept the Data):** If the day didn't go according to plan, the goal is not to get frustrated. The goal is to accept the new information. The blueprint was a hypothesis; your actions tested it.

- **Refocus (Refine the Blueprint):** Based on the feedback, how do you need to adjust the plan for tomorrow? This is the heart of the daily design process.

- **Relaunch (Prepare for the Next Start):** Define your "Primary Investment" for tomorrow. This ensures you wake up with a clear target.

The BUILD Strategy - Laying Your Daily Bricks

The Core Principle: Your Daily Actions Are Your Legacy

If DEFINE is your "why" and DESIGN is your "how," then BUILD is your "now." Your daily actions are your legacy. A magnificent cathedral is the sum of a million small, perfectly placed stones. A fulfilling life is built in the succession of a thousand small, consistent, and courageous daily choices. The world will not remember you for the blueprint you designed, but for the structure you built. Your legacy is not the intention in your mind; it is the evidence of the work you do with your hands.

This is the phase where you transform from planner to practitioner. It is where you close the "knowing-doing gap." The conveyor-belt mindset waits for perfect conditions. The architect understands that the only guarantee is the one you create through your own effort. There are no neutral days. Every 24-hour cycle is a step toward your vision or a step away from it. This is not meant to create pressure, but to instill a profound sense of purpose in the ordinary moments of your life. Your daily routine is your construction schedule.

Key Concepts Revisited: To be an effective builder, you must carry three critical mindsets to the construction site. **Pursue Progress, Not Perfection.** Your goal each day is not to lay a "perfect" brick, but to lay a brick. **Failure as an Ingredient.** A failed action is not a verdict on your ability; it is a valuable lesson in what doesn't work. **Overcoming Disappointment.** Your ability to manage the emotional fallout of setbacks is critical. Use the "Recognize & Release, Retrieve Feedback, and Reset & Relaunch" toolkit.

The Essential Tools & Systems:

- **The Architect Hour & Time Blocking:** These are the foundational systems that create the time and space for construction.

- **The Rule of Three:** This is your system for maintaining focus and avoiding overwhelm.

- **The Smallest Viable Action (SVA):** This is your master tool for breaking inertia and overcoming procrastination.

Daily Integration: Laying Your "Daily Brick"

This is the culmination of your entire strategy. It is the moment where the abstract concepts of vision and design become the undeniable, physical reality of a brick being laid. This is where the talk stops and the work begins. Do not underestimate the power of this simple, daily act. A single brick may seem insignificant against the backdrop of a grand skyscraper, but it is the only thing that is real. The blueprint is a promise; the brick is the proof. Laying your Daily Brick is more than a task on a to-do list; it is a daily vote you cast for your future self. It is a physical declaration that you are a builder. It is the engine of your self-confidence, the tangible evidence that you are a person who does what they say they will do. This is how you build a legacy not by dreaming of a distant future, but by winning the day, today, with the simple, focused, and powerful act of laying one well-chosen brick.

Actionable Habit: Pay Yourself First with you Daily Brick

Frame the "Primary Investment" you identify in your morning Architect Hour as your **"Daily Brick."** The protected "Blueprint Time" in your schedule is the time you have reserved to lay that one brick with focus and excellence. This is how you make the grand process of "building a life" as simple and actionable as laying one brick each day.

1. You wake up and perform your **DEFINE** strategy with the "Two-Minute Anchor."

2. During your Architect Hour, you identify your Daily Brick.

3. You look at your **DESIGNED** schedule and see the "Blueprint Time" you've created.

4. When that time arrives, you enter the **BUILD** phase. You eliminate distractions and lay your Daily Brick.

5. In your evening Architect Hour, you review the day's work, refining the design for tomorrow.

The Architect's Commitment - A Lifelong Practice

The true mastery of a life architect lies in understanding that Define, Design, and Build are not a linear process. They are not three separate stages you complete in order. It is a continuous, dynamic, and virtuous cycle that you will engage in for the rest of your life. Think of it as an upward spiral. The first turn of the wheel may feel slow, heavy, and clumsy. Your first vision may be blurry, your first blueprint may be flawed, and your first attempts at building may be awkward. This is not a sign of failure; it is the sign of a beginner. But with each rotation, the wheel gains momentum.

You start by **Defining** your vision. This informs the **Design** of your blueprint. Your blueprint dictates the **Building** you do. But here is the magic: the act of building provides you with the most valuable feedback. In your evening review, you use this data to refine your **Design**. A more intelligent design, in turn, can lead to new insights. As you build and learn, you may discover a new strength or a more meaningful problem to solve. This new information feeds back into the **Define** phase, allowing you to clarify and even elevate your original vision. A bigger, clearer vision then demands a more sophisticated design, which demands more skillful building. This is the cycle. *Build >> Reframe Design >> Elevate Definition >> Build Better*. It is the engine of continuous growth, the process by which you find the *Next You*, again and again.

This book and the field guide within it are not the source of your power; they are simply a mirror reflecting the power that was always within you. The frameworks and strategies are not a magic formula; they are a set of tools designed to help you excavate, shape, and build with the potential you already possess. You now have a complete, integrated system for intentional life design. You have the mindsets to weather the internal storms, the tools to bring structure to your ambition, and the systems to translate your vision into daily actions. There are no more excuses. The responsibility and the magnificent opportunity are entirely yours.

Do not make the mistake of placing this book on a shelf to collect dust. Inspiration without implementation is a delusion. It is the cheapest form of lazy ambition, the feeling of progress without the effort. The journey of Finding The Next You does not start tomorrow or when you feel ready. A sense of readiness is not a prerequisite for starting; it is the *result* of starting. It is the confidence you build brick by brick. Your journey begins with your very next choice. The choice to get out of your head. The choice to pursue progress, not perfection. The choice to schedule your Architect Hour for tomorrow morning. The choice to identify your first Daily Brick.

You are standing on your construction site. Your blueprint is in your hand. The first brick is at your feet. Pick it up and go to work. This work is not a one-time action, but a continuous commitment to building.

Chapter 13

The Architect You Must Become

The Final Question

You have the blueprint in your hands and the tools in your belt. You understand the strategy of the build. But a blueprint, no matter how brilliant, is just ink on paper. It requires a builder to breathe life into it. It requires a builder to breathe life into it. The strategies and systems in this book are your tools, but *you* are the architect. The quality of the final structure will ultimately be determined not by the plans themselves, but by the character, resilience, and identity of the one holding them.

This brings us to the final, and most important, question of our entire journey. It is a question that transitions us from the "what" and the "how" to the "who." **Who is the person that will deploy these tools?** Who is the one that will show up to the construction site day after day, especially when the initial excitement fades and the real work begins?

This final chapter is not about what you need to *do*; you have those instructions. This is about who you need to *become*. Finding The Next You is an evolution, not a reinvention. "Reinventing yourself" often comes from a place of deficit, the idea that who you are today is fundamentally flawed. That is the logic of the conveyor belt. The architect mindset is radically different. It is not about fixing something broken; it is about building upon the unique foundation of who you already are. It is a declaration that the person you are today is worthy and capable of building an extraordinary future. You are integrating the wisdom of your past with the ambition of your future to become the person you were always meant to be.

The Identity of a Builder

The most profound shift you will make is not in your schedule, but in your self-concept. To sustain this work for a lifetime, you must move beyond simply *acting* like a builder; you must adopt the **identity of a builder**. You are not someone who *wants* to build a better life; you are a builder, and building a better life is simply what you do.

You must become the person whose internal belief is louder than the external chorus of doubt. When you stepped off the conveyor belt, you stepped out of the system of external validation. There are no more grades, no more standardized promotions. In the world of the architect, the only validation that truly matters is the one that comes from within. As you begin to build, the voices of doubt will inevitably appear. They will come from well-meaning friends and family made uncomfortable by your choice to forge your own path. Their skepticism is not a reflection of your capability; it is a reflection of their own fear. You must learn to see their disbelief not as a verdict on your vision, but as a distraction from your work.

You must become the person who understands that your success does not require a co-signer. The vision for your life was given to you. It is your responsibility to build it. Seeking the approval of others before you begin is like asking them to co-sign a loan for a house they cannot see. You do not waste precious energy trying to convince the world with words. You understand that your job is to build. You let the tangible evidence of the bricks you lay become the only argument that matters.

Consumer Identity vs. Architect Identity

To fully inhabit this new identity, you must understand how it differs from the default setting of the world around you. The shift from Consumer to Architect is not just a professional change; it is a total operating system upgrade that affects every domain of your life.

In Your Career:
- **The Consumer** views a job as a transaction: time traded for money. They wait for instructions, seek to meet the minimum requirements to avoid being fired, and look for the path of least resistance. They ask, "What can this company give me?"

- **The Architect** views a career as a craft. They view their role, no matter the title, as a place to solve problems and create value. They do not wait for a map; they chart the course. They ask, "What can I build here, and what skills can I extract from this experience to fuel my larger blueprint?"

In Your Relationships:

- **The Consumer** approaches relationships with a "what have you done for me lately?" mindset. They consume the energy of others, looking for people to validate them or entertain them.

- **The Architect** builds relationships. They invest in others, understanding that a strong network is a structure of mutual support. They seek out "iron sharpens iron" connections, looking for people who challenge them to grow, not just those who make them feel comfortable.

In Your Finances:

- **The Consumer** uses money to buy status symbols or temporary distractions. They spend to signal success to others.

- **The Architect** uses money as a tool for construction. They "pay themselves first" not just to hoard cash, but to buy freedom. They invest in their own education, their tools, and their experiences. They spend to build capacity.

The Imposter Syndrome Tax

As you adopt this new identity, you will inevitably encounter a formidable enemy: Imposter Syndrome. This is the voice that whispers, "Who are you to build this? You're a fraud. Everyone is going to find out you don't know what you're doing."

The conveyor-belt mindset tells you that Imposter Syndrome is a stop sign. It says that if you feel like an imposter, you must be doing something wrong. The Architect knows the truth: Imposter Syndrome is not a stop sign; it is a tax on growth. It is the fee you pay for entering a room you have never been in before. If you never feel like an imposter, it simply means you are not stretching yourself. You are staying in the safe, small rooms of your past.

The person you must become learns to flip the script on this feeling. When the voice says, "You don't know what you're doing," the Architect replies, "Correct. I am a learner. And I am currently learning how to do this." You shift your identity from "Expert" (which is fragile and easily threatened) to "Builder" (which is resilient and growth-oriented). An expert has to know everything; a builder just has to figure out the next step.

The Architect's Hub: Your Design Studio is your Creative Fortress.

You cannot design a new life while standing in the middle of your old one. Identity is shaped by environment and reinforced by community. Just as a master craftsman needs a workshop, you need a dedicated space to forge your new identity. This is the purpose of

The Architect's Hub. The Hub is two things simultaneously: a physical workspace and a communal connection.

First, it is your **Individual Workspace**. This is the physical manifestation of your commitment to yourself. It doesn't have to be a corner office; it can be a desk in your bedroom or a specific table at a library. But it must be *yours*. It is the space where you enter the "deep work" zone, where you shut out the noise of the conveyor belt and commune with your blueprint. When you sit in this space, your brain should immediately signal: *We are building now.* This physical boundary protects your mental focus and reinforces your identity as a creator.

Second, and perhaps more importantly, it is your **Community of fellow Architects**. The myth of being "self-made" is dangerous. No significant structure is built by a single pair of hands. While the vision is yours, the build requires a crew. The Architect's Hub is where you connect with other builders people who are also stepping off the conveyor belt, also facing the fear of the blank page, and also committed to the process of becoming.

Engaging in this community strengthens your identity in profound ways. When you are alone, the doubts in your head can sound like the truth. But when you are in a community of builders, you realize those doubts are universal. You see others pushing through the same barriers, which gives you permission and courage to push through yours. You share your small wins and have them celebrated by people who understand the effort they took. You share your setbacks and receive strategy instead of pity.

In the Hub, you are not the "crazy one" for wanting more than the status quo; you are the normal one. This normalization of ambition is critical. You become the average of the people you spend the most time with. If you spend your time with passengers, you will remain a passenger. If you spend your time in the Hub with other Architects, you will inevitably become one.

The Confidence Loop:
Produce, Deliver, Measure, Repeat

One of the greatest lies of the conveyor-belt mindset is that confidence is a personality trait you either are born with or are not. It creates a paralyzing catch-22: "I can't start until I feel confident, but I can't feel confident until I start." The architect rejects this myth. You must understand a fundamental truth: **Confidence is not a prerequisite for building; it is the result of building.**

Confidence is not a feeling you wait for; it is a structure you build. It is the tangible, undeniable evidence of your own capability, earned through a disciplined and repeatable process called **The Confidence Loop**.

- **Stage 1: Courageous Action (Produce):** Everything begins with a choice to act in the presence of fear. Courage is the currency you use to pay the entry fee. You ignore the skyscraper and focus only on the first, tiny, manageable brick.

- **Stage 2: Consistent Output (Deliver):** Motivation is fleeting; systems are reliable. To "deliver" means to consistently produce your planned output regardless of how you feel. Each day you honor this commitment, you are adding a layer to the foundation of your own reliability.

- **Stage 3: Honest Assessment (Measure):** You step back and assess the work with a clear, dispassionate eye. You do not ask, "Am I a failure?" You ask, "Did this brick fit?"

- **Stage 4: Intelligent Adaptation (Repeat):** Based on the feedback, you refine your approach and go again.

With every turn of this cycle, you manufacture authentic, unshakable self-confidence. You are building a "Confidence Résumé", a private record of your own courage.

Case Study: Sarah's Pivot

To understand how this loop functions in the real world, let's look at Sarah. Sarah is a 26-year-old marketing coordinator who feels the "Triple Disconnect" acutely. She is good at her job, but she feels empty. Her blueprint reveals a deep desire to move into User Experience (UX) Design, a field where she can use psychology and creativity to solve problems. But she has no degree in design, no portfolio, and a mountain of Imposter Syndrome.

The Trap: The conveyor-belt mindset tells Sarah she needs to go back to grad school for two years before she can even call herself a designer. She freezes, overwhelmed by the size of the leap.

The Loop in Action:

- **Produce (Courageous Action):** Sarah uses the "Smallest Viable Action" concept. She doesn't apply to grad school. Instead, she finds a free 1-hour tutorial on Figma (design software) and commits to watching it on Tuesday night. It's a tiny, non-threatening action. She does it. *Receipt: Courage.*

- **Deliver (Consistent Output):** She sets a "Daily Brick" in her Architect Hour: "Replicate one app screen design every evening for 30 minutes." She does this for two weeks. Some days the designs look terrible; some days they look okay. But she shows up. She is proving to herself that she is disciplined. *Receipt: Reliability.*

- **Measure (Honest Assessment):** After two weeks, she looks at her folder of 14 designs. She realizes she loves the logic of the layout but hates picking color palettes. This is critical data. She isn't failing; she is learning her preferences. She asks a friend in tech for feedback. The friend says, "Your layouts are great, but your visual style is dated." *Receipt: Data.*

- **Repeat (Intelligent Adaptation):** Sarah doesn't quit. She adapts. She realizes her strength is in *UX Research and Wireframing*, not visual UI design. She adjusts her blueprint. Her next "Produce" cycle focuses on finding a course specifically for UX Research.

Six months later, Sarah hasn't just "learned" about UX; she has built a portfolio of wireframes. She has the confidence to apply for jobs not because she hyped herself up in the mirror, but because she has a stack of receipts proving she can do the work. She built her confidence loop by loop.

Breaking the Loop of Inaction

There will be times when the Confidence Loop feels jammed. You know what you need to do, but you are frozen. This is the "Freeze Response," your nervous system's way of protecting you from a perceived threat.

When you are stuck in the loop of inaction, you cannot think your way out. You can only act your way out. This is where the **Smallest Viable Action (SVA)** becomes your emergency tool. When you cannot bring yourself to write the chapter, write one sentence. When you cannot bring yourself to go to the gym, put on your workout clothes.

The goal of the SVA is not progress; it is to restart the engine. It is a hack for your nervous system that proves to your brain the threat isn't real. Once you take that microscopic action, the loop unlocks. You produce, you deliver, and suddenly, you are back in motion. The Architect knows that momentum is a renewable resource, and action is the spark that ignites it.

Character Over Tactics: Embracing the Process

In Chapter 10, we discussed the *tactics* of handling failure and disappointment. Now, we must discuss the *character* required to welcome them. The person you must become understands that the ultimate prize is not the finished skyscraper. The prize is the person you become while building it.

The conveyor-belt mindset is obsessed with the destination ("I'll be happy when..."). The architect falls in love with the process. You must fundamentally change your relationship with the very things the world has taught you to avoid.

- **Fear is Your Compass:** Fear is not a signal to stop; it is a signal that you are at the edge of your comfort zone, the only place where real growth occurs. You utilize fear as a compass, pointing directly toward the next action you need to take to evolve.

- **Failure is Your Tutor:** You do not just tolerate failure; you respect it. A master builder becomes a master by making thousands of mistakes and meticulously learning from every single one. You stop taking failure personally and start taking it professionally.

- **Disappointment is Your Test:** Disappointment is the emotional tax on ambition. The person you must become learns to see disappointment not as a reason to quit, but as a test of your commitment to your vision. It is the moment where you decide if your "why" is strong enough to withstand a setback.

The world celebrates the public victory. But the architect finds deep satisfaction in the **private victory**. The private victory is the quiet, unseen work of the ordinary day. When you show up for your "Blueprint Time" on a day you feel tired and uninspired, you have won a private victory. These moments forge your self-confidence from the inside out.

The Choice to Build a Legacy

The gap between your potential and your reality is now a choice. It is not a matter of your economic class, your background, or some innate talent you were or were not born with. Success is not a birthright, reserved for a chosen few. It is a choice, available to all who are willing to make it. The conveyor-belt world thrives on the myth of limitation. It tells you that your future is predetermined by your past by your zip code, your family's income, your GPA. It wants you to believe that you need permission to succeed, that you must wait for an external gatekeeper to anoint you as "worthy."

The architect knows this is a lie. You do not need permission. You do not need a lucky break. You need to make a decision. It is the decision that success will be yours, not because you are owed it, but because you will build it. It is the choice to close the gap not by waiting for the world to pull you across, but by building a bridge, one daily brick at a time. This decision is the most powerful force in the universe. It is the moment you stop being a victim of your circumstances and become the creator of your circumstances. You have the blueprint. You have the tools. The gap is no longer an obstacle; it is the construction site. The choice to build is the only thing that matters.

The Ripple Effect

But why does this choice matter so profoundly? It matters because your choice is never isolated. When you choose to build, you are not just constructing a life for yourself; you are constructing a legacy for everyone who comes after you. This is the ultimate maturity of the architect: the realization that the purpose of the skyscraper is not just to touch the sky, but to provide shelter, opportunity, and inspiration for others.

We often think of legacy as something we leave behind when we are gone, a static monument to our past. But for the architect, legacy is a dynamic force created in the present. It is built through the accumulation of your daily choices. This is **The Ripple Effect**.

Imagine your life as a stone dropped into a still pond. The first splash is your personal success the skills you build, the career you design, the peace you find. But that splash inevitably creates waves that travel outward.

The First Circle: Your immediate family and friends. When you choose courage over comfort, you are modeling bravery for your children. You are showing them that a life of passion is possible. When you break a generational cycle of poverty, addiction, or limitation, you are changing the starting line for your entire lineage. You are paying a "success tax" so they don't have to. Your blueprint becomes their proof of concept.

The Second Circle: Your industry and profession. This is where your professional standards become a beacon. When you build a business with integrity, you raise the ethical bar for your entire market. When you mentor a junior colleague, you accelerate their growth and create a future leader. By operating as an Architect in a world of Consumers, you disrupt the status quo of your field. You prove that it is possible to succeed without compromising your values, giving permission to your peers to question the conveyor belt they are on.

The Third Circle: Your community and society. This is the widest ripple, where your success transforms into civic contribution. Consider the impact of Andrew Carnegie, whom we discussed earlier. His choice to educate himself didn't just lift him out of poverty; it built libraries that lifted millions. Your blueprint has the same potential. You may not build libraries, but you can create libraries of possibility in the minds of those you touch. Whether through philanthropy, volunteerism, or simply being a stabilizing force in your neighborhood, your individual construction project becomes a cornerstone for the community's well-being.

The Architect's Generosity

This leads to the final evolution of your identity: **The Architect's Generosity.** The conveyor belt operates on a **Scarcity Mindset**. It views success as a fixed pie; if you take a slice, there is less for me. This breeds competition, hoarding, and fear. It keeps people in their boxes, guarding their small patch of territory.

The Architect operates on an **Abundance Mindset**. You understand that success is not a pie to be divided, but a candle to be shared. Lighting another candle does not diminish your own flame; it only makes the room brighter. The Architect builds with an open hand. You build your career (Success) so that you can mentor others (Significance). You build your wealth (Success) so that you can invest in your community (Significance). You build your character (Success) so that you can be a rock for those who are struggling (Significance).

This transforms the nature of your "Daily Brick." When you are tired, when the work is hard, when you want to quit, remember that you are not just laying a brick for yourself. You are laying a foundation for others to stand on. You are lowering a ladder for those still stuck in the pit you climbed out of.

The choice to succeed is a choice to serve. It is a choice to matter. This is the architecture of legacy, moving from the selfish ambition of "what can I get?" to the noble ambition of "what can I build for others?" When you view your blueprint through this lens, the burden of the work becomes lighter because the purpose of the work has become greater.

The Final Charge

You began this book as a passenger on a conveyor belt. Along the way, you have awakened to your own power. You have become the architect. You now possess a toolkit that can transform any idea in your mind into a reality in the world. The question is no longer *if* you can build the life you desire, but *if* you *will*.

Therefore, the final charge of this book is not simply to "go build." That is the work of a laborer. Your calling is higher. The final charge is to **go become**.

"Go become" the person whose internal belief is louder than the external chorus of doubt.

"Go become" the person who finds joy in the journey, not just the prize of the destination.

"Go become" the person who treats failure not as a verdict, but as a tutor.

"Go become" the person who consistently wins the private victory of the ordinary day.

This is the lifelong commitment of the architect: to always be evolving into the person capable of building the next, more ambitious structure on your blueprint. Do not let this book become another source of inspiration that fades with time. Let it be the ignition switch. The journey of Finding The Next You does not start tomorrow, next week, or when the conditions are perfect. Those are the excuses of those that wait for permission and the approval of others before they believe in themselves and pursue their calling to live a purposeful and fulfilling life. The architect knows that the journey starts the moment you decide it does.

So what are you waiting on?

Its your time to become, to find the next you and build your way forward to live the life you envision.

THE ARCHITECT'S HUB: TOOL GLOSSARY

This glossary serves as your index to the Architect's Hub, your Digital Design Studio. Each tool listed below corresponds to a specific phase of the Define, Design, Build framework found in the book. To access these dynamic resources, simply enter the URL provided into your browser or scan the below QR code.

Phase 1: DEFINE

Establishing your vision and starting coordinates.

1. Blueprint for Success Assessment

- **Book Location:** Chapter 5 *Your New Title: "The Architect"*

- Description: Before you can build, you must assess your readiness. This diagnostic tool measures your current standing across the three key coordinates of the Architect's mindset: Self-Confidence, Persistence, and Continuous Learning. It provides a customized report outlining your strengths and identifying the specific opportunities for improvement you need to address before breaking ground on your new life.

- **Access URL:** FindingTheNextYou.com/assess

2. Personal GPS Calibration

- **Book Location:** Chapter 6 *Building Your GPS to Success*

- **Description:** You cannot navigate to a new destination if you don't know where you are standing right now. This tool helps you pinpoint your "You Are Here" dot. It guides you through a rigorous inventory of your current reality, auditing your Power Skills, internal beliefs, environmental influences, and available resources (time, energy, money). It converts vague feelings of "being stuck" into clear, actionable data points.

- **Access URL:** FindingTheNextYou.com/gps

Phase 2: DESIGN

Drafting the plans and creating the systems.

3. The Architect's Hub (Main Studio Entry)

- **Book Location:** Chapter 7 *The Architect's Hub: Your Design Studio*

- **Description:** This is the master gateway to your Digital Design Studio. It is the central workspace where all other tools live. Think of this as walking into your professional office, a distraction-free sanctuary designed to foster focus, build community with fellow Architects, and provide the specific instruments you need to turn your vision into a blueprint.

- **Access URL:** FindingTheNextYou.com/start

4. The One-Page Blueprint

- **Book Location:** Chapter 8 *Creating Your Blueprint*

- Description: This is your master plan. It synthesizes your vision, values, and strategy into a single, powerful document. This digital tool walks you through the four-step drafting process: writing your "Future Self" letter, defining your Three Pillars (core values), sourcing your Materials Inventory (skills/relationships needed), and identifying your First Brick. It transforms your abstract dreams into a tangible construction document.

- **Access URL:** FindingTheNextYou.com/Blueprint

5. The Time Audit

- **Book Location:** Chapter 9 *Rebuild Your Routine*

- Description: Time is your most valuable, non-renewable construction material. This tool helps you conduct a forensic analysis of where your 24 hours actually go. It exposes the "Drift Time" lost to low-value activities and helps you identify the hidden inventory of hours you can reclaim to invest in your blueprint. It is the prerequisite for building your "Pay Yourself First" schedule.

- **Access URL:** FindingTheNextYou.com/Time

Phase 3: BUILD

Executing the work and refining the structure.

6. Skill Builder Tool

- **Book Location:** Chapter 11 *The Architect's Diet* (Also referenced in Chapter 7)

- Description: The Architect is a continuous learner. This tool operationalizes your growth by helping you create a "Skill Development Plan." Instead of random learning, this tracker helps you identify the specific "Power Skills" your blueprint requires, source the best materials (books, courses, podcasts), and schedule the time to acquire them. It turns you from a passive consumer of information into an active curator of knowledge.

- **Access URL:** FindingTheNextYou.com/skills

7. Consumption Diet Audit

- **Book Location:** Chapter 11 *The Architect's Diet*

- Description: "Garbage in, garbage out" applies to your mind as much as your body. This audit tool helps you track your information intake over a 3-day period. It categorizes your consumption into "Entertainment" (anesthetic) vs. "Education" (fuel), giving you a clear ratio of whether you are feeding your distractions or your dreams. It is the first step in curating an environment that supports your growth.

- **Access URL:** FindingTheNextYou.com/diet